THURSDAY IS MISSING

Richard Passmore

THURSDAY
IS
MISSING

RICHARD PASSMORE

Thomas Harmsworth Publishing
London

By the same author:
Blenheim Boy
Moving Tent

© 1984 Richard Passmore

First published 1984

This book was written largely on
the insistence of three dear friends:
Jim Brown
Rose Dumbleton
Rhoda Harley.
I offer it to them gladly.

ISBN 0 9506012 7 6

Printed in Great Britain by
The Pitman Press, Bath

Preface

Memory seems to tell me that these things indeed happened: that on such an occasion I was sad or amused or lonely or frightened. But something closer to me than memory refuses to accept that all this happened to *me*. True, it answered to somebody answering to my name, using the forerunner of this body through which I still experience a full and happy life. Yet the someone to whom these things happened did not think or feel as I do now – and so, clearly, he was not me. Whoever he was, I am grateful to him.

The years of my childhood were rich in many-sided experience. Our material poverty was relieved by mutual help and the ugliness of our surroundings by occasional glimpses of beauty. Looking back now I cannot say that those early years were either happy or unhappy: but they were certainly full.

Here is an account of my childhood. The years of my manhood I have already described elsewhere.

Richard Passmore

Thanks are due to R E Benbow Esq, to Mrs M Ben Mousa, to the staff of the Liverpool Record Office and to the Boys' Brigade for assistance with illustrations. Messrs Chappell's have kindly given permission to quote from *Maytime*.

1

'I want meat, meat, meat.'

Whenever, reluctantly, I had to share my weekly bath with Dorothy, I insisted adamantly that she should sit at the plug end, with her head against the taps. After all, as I pointed out, it was *my* house, not hers, and it was bad enough that I might not bath alone: it mattered not that she was a guest nor that ladies took precedence. As I was usually an amenable child, this weekly act of self-assertion was generally tolerated, so that I sat at the comfortable end; true, there was a less-than-comfortable confusion of legs and, particularly, feet – whichever way we sought to arrange them. However, once in the bath we largely ignored each other: when she had taken her clothes off, you would not have known that she was merely a girl. Our house, by the way, was the only one in the block with a bathroom, the neighbours making do with galvanised hip-baths (as we had to do at some time during most winters, when the pipes froze). The shared bath was my own unwilling contribution, therefore, to neighbourly help.

(Some years ago I was paying one of my infrequent visits to Liverpool and one evening was reminiscing with a friend. Dorothy was mentioned and he told me her present whereabouts, so a day or two later I paid her a call. She lived, it seemed, in the usual suburban semi, neat and trim and with a well-tended garden. Curious to know whether she would recognise me, I rang the bell. When the door opened a man looked at me rather suspiciously; he was much my own age and had, I noted, tattooed forearms – always a bad sign.

He said, 'Yes?'

I said, 'Is Mrs Harris in?'

The suspicion deepened; he asked, 'Do you know my wife?'

Some devil possessed me. I replied, 'Oh yes. We used to bath together.'

His mouth opened to say something, hung open, closed again. He stared at me in some confusion. Again his mouth half-opened but closed once more. Without another word he suddenly turned around and went back into the house. Soon Dorothy appeared, wiping her hands on a tea-towel: her eyes glinted behind her spectacles just as they had done so many years before. Recognition was instantaneous and soon we were sitting over the inevitable cup of tea. But her husband, clearly, did not consider that the episode had been at all funny.)

The bath was a weekly occasion: we could not afford – or even see the necessity – to heat up the water more frequently. During the course of the evening all the family used the same water, diluted and warmed by successive libations from the large and sooty kettle which lived on the hob of the old-fashioned kitchen-range in the living-room or, at long intervals, from the tap proper. The bathwater became steadily more opaque as the evening wore on. When your ration of time was up, you were extracted from the warmth and into the cooler air, wrapped protesting and shivering in a bath-towel, slung over mother's shoulder and carried downstairs; there you stood in front of the fire and were briskly rubbed-down. Then came the torture and often tears of a comb pulled through tangled hair before you were allowed to dress again, ready for bed. We knew neither pyjamas nor nightshirt: for bed we simply removed outer clothing – jersey, trousers, socks and shoes – and rolled in. Looking back now I can see how early my life was conditioned, and my values and standards were shaped, by poverty. Nevertheless, in those very early days life was still happy: the bad days were yet to come.

Happiness was mainly being close to Mum: watching her, hearing her singing as she went about some household task or ran lightly up and down the stairs, being frequently picked up and

2

loved, spoken to, put down. Happiness was sitting up against the living-room window while Mum, outside in the paved backyard, cleaned the window with a broom and a pail of soapy water and finally threw another pail of clean water over the soapy glass. Happiness was waiting for the enchanted moment when transparency diminished to translucency as little waves ran momentarily down the glass and then vanished, to reveal that well-loved face laughing in at us. Then there was an answering chortle of glee, the warmth of love renewed and confidence justified.

I must, then, have been very young: indeed, I had not started school. Was I perhaps four – or even three? Certainly I now had a brother two and a half years younger; his name was Bob. The family called him Bunty, a name which he often resented. To tease him we would often sing a little ditty:

> Baby, Baby Bunting,
> Daddy's gone ahunting –
> Gone to get a rabbit-skin
> To wrap his Baby Bunting in.

This chorus was usually enough to provoke an outburst of mixed tears and temper; it is long since we sang it and indeed I would not now advise it: Bunty is now all of six feet three and some fifteen stone. My sister Betty had not yet been born. We had, indeed, a Daddy, but only technically – we knew nothing of him. He was a sailor, a ship's cook, and away from home for a year or eighteen months at a time. Occasionally a tall, sallow stranger arrived and sat in Daddy's chair, stayed a week or two and vanished again. Then Mum would be inexplicably tearful but it was clear to me that with his going the family was once again complete. Every such visit meant a wickerwork hamper of grapefruit – unknown at that time in the shops of our working-class neighbourhood; there would be, too, hands of green bananas hanging around the canary's cage, slowly ripening. The bird, perhaps stirred by some racial memory, would throb with passionate song, often with half-extended wings, quivering. Bonzo, our mainly-fox-terrier

3

mongrel, also seemed to miss the stranger: he would come into the room, look hopefully at that chair, whine a little, lower his tail back into its slot, and lie down in his favourite spot on the carpet, before the fire.

On fine days my mother would put Bob into his push-chair; I would walk alongside, one hand obediently clamped to the frame, and we would set out for the Botanic Gardens. At that time huge and floppy hats were in vogue and I clearly remember my mother's favourite skirt, with semi-concealed red panels; she wore Russian boots: a kind of leather Wellington with concertina-type wrinkles just above the ankles. I wore my favourite sailor-suit, with HMS *Centaur* on the hatband. Later I would offer determined resistance to having this finery removed: I would happily have slept in it.

The Gardens offered neat gravel paths and carefully-cultivated flower-beds set in well-kept lawns ('Keep off the Grass. Penalty for infringement Forty Shillings'). There were long hot-houses, with (I think) fuchsias which made a pleasant pop when squeezed and, greatest thrill of the day, a murky pond in which could be glimpsed jacksharps, careless and free in their twilit and squamous world. Odd that I never joined the Navy, nor did I take up fishing. On the way home we would walk back up Edge Lane, then lined with prosperous houses, each with its own arc of carriage drive curving around a well-kept lawn to an imposing entrance. Trees overhung the pavement and cast dappled shadows: the trick was to maintain the obligatory handhold on the pushchair and yet step only in the bright patches between the flickering shadows. And it was always here that we performed the ritual chant without which the day would not have been complete. Mother would ask us to speculate on what there would be for tea; there would always be bread and jam, of course, (I was addicted to blackcurrant) and cake, but invariably I would chant, 'I don't want cake, cake, cake. I want meat, meat, meat.' In later years my mother would recount this to me and it was clear, quite clear, that those were the happiest days of her life. I am still a great meat-eater.

We lived, and I was born, in 93 Hall Lane – which is still standing. Hall Lane was the only tarmac road in an area of

4

cobblestones, and it ran along the brow of a hill. Opposite our house the land fell away and we could see over the roofs of central Liverpool to the towers and clocks of the Liver Buildings. The noise of shipping in the Mersey came clearly to us and was an unregarded part of the background of everyday life. On foggy days the air would be filled with mournful boomings from the bigger ships – in those days the transatlantic liners still used the port – and shrill pipings from the smaller ferries and coasters. Daily we checked our clocks by the one o'clock gun, fired from the Perch Rock Battery at New Brighton, some miles down the river and then still a busy and brightly-painted holiday resort. Alas, national prosperity killed New Brighton: the clientele which would once have enjoyed its attractions and found them within their means now go further afield, to the Costa Whateveritis.

The downward slope from Hall Lane was crowded with squalid streets: opposite the house was Bengel Street, followed by Warburton, Tillotson, Crossley, Horsley, Dodderidge and Bunyan Streets. After whom were they named, I wonder? On the corner of each street was a pub: however poor the people and whatever the family went short of, there was always money for the poor man's panacea, beer. At the bottom end of Hall Lane was Low Hill Post Office, on the corner of a main traffic artery, Kensington, along which the trams rattled and swayed on their journeys down to the Pier Head (the focal point for almost all routes) and out to Old Swan and Knotty Ash and Prescot. A penny ticket would take you all the way. Opposite the Post Office was a place of mystery, the Catholic church of the Sacred Heart; foreboding and fear surrounded it and nothing would have induced us children of the area to set foot in it. True, some of our friends were catholics and regularly attended a sinister rite known as Mass, but our feelings were well expressed by the occasional Orange Lodges, who always saluted the church with an intensified banging of their drums and the chanting of a traditional ditty: 'Aye, aye, Paddy was a bastard, Paddy was a bastard, aye, aye, aye.' At the other end of the Lane was Mount Vernon Green, triangular and trim, with a central fountain which played on summer days. The

5

Green was perfection: not a blade of grass, not a flower out of place. The Green remained immaculate because it was surrounded by a spiked fence; since that fence was removed, during the last war, the place has become a trodden slum.*

Further on again was Edge Lane, and at the junction with Hall Lane was Towerlands Street, a tight curve enclosing Saint Mary's Church. All day and for most of the night we would hear clearly the metal wheels of the trams screaming their torment as they negotiated that over-steep curve; the wonder was that so evident a strain did not tear the wheels off. The church stood in its own raised God's Acre, an outpost of the vanished countryside, now invested by the remorseless wen. Then came the downward slope of Erskine Street and Paddington. One day a tram lumbered down Paddington, out of control, its frantic driver beating out a staccato warning on his foot-bell. At the bottom of the steep slope the tram failed to negotiate the sharp bend, left the rails and ploughed across the road and mounted the pavement, to crash on to its side in a welter of glass, metal, shopfront, prams and people. It was the only serious tram accident that I can ever remember: the trams were peaceful, clumsy, noisy mammoths, cheaply transporting the urban proletariat. From the top deck or, more excitingly, from the open balconies at each end you had a God's eye view of crowded pavements, busy shops, house interiors. Out in the suburbs the trams ran on grassy enclosures down the centre of the road, with low hedges on each side. Here, mysteriously, the noise was abated and they hissed along in a fascinating way. The modern trams, the Green Goddesses which came along in the thirties, were never quite the same: quieter they were, yes, and smoother, and fully-enclosed – but something had been lost. Trams were inextricably part of my childhood. Chiefly, I suppose, I remember the Illuminated Car, well worthy of its capitals. The sides were huge fields of electric bulbs on which unknown artists constructed magical patterns in coloured light – often the municipal coat of arms. On the open top deck a band, invisible behind that radiance,

* The fence has been restored, I find, with a corresponding improvement.

6

played for us. Is heaven itself hidden from us by the glory of its own radiance. I wonder? The Tram would process – no lesser word is adequate – to Lime Street, where it would be parked in a siding between the entrance to the Station on the one side and Professor Codman's Punch and Judy show on the other, the brilliance illuminating the tall columns of Saint George's Hall. Inside sat a few fortunate, unspeakably-privileged mortals. On special occasions the tram came out from its shed, next to Wavertree Park, to delight the citizenry, and on its return, late at night, it would pass up the recently-laid line in North View, separated from our bedroom only by the Green. The extravagance of light would pluck us out of our shared bed like hooked fish; mute with wonder we would watch, glorying in every full second, and then scamper back to bed and snuggle down, turning over and over the memory of that unexpected bonus.

People. Life was always full of people: my mother would have shamed Abou ben Adhem himself. Lacking in family contacts, she made the world her family. Her own family, to which I owe much of my heredity, lived in farthest Cornwall, in and near to a village called Tywardreath. Sometimes Mother would babble of her girl-hood; her voice would become wistful and her eyes were far away as she spoke of Newquay, of Bedruthan Steps and Fowey and Par. She would sing the Floral Dance. Alas, Cornwall was three hundred miles away; it might as well have been in another continent, so utterly impossible was it for us to go there or to see our grandparents. Grandfather had been a railway lengthman but had become blind, so was equally unable to visit us, but was still a Wesleyan lay preacher. In the spring of each year would come through the post a metal sandwich box; inside, packed in moss, would be a tangle of primroses, beautiful, fresh, sweet-smelling. They were the earnest of a legend, the substance of things hoped for, the evidence of things not seen. One day, I resolved, I should go to Cornwall – a resolution to be added to a growing total. 'Beware of what you wish for in your youth,' admonished Goethe, 'for in your middle age it will surely come true.' Many resolutions – most of them – have indeed come true and I have had cause to

7

regret none. Divine Providence, surely, saw to it that the resolutions which I made even in my infancy were wholesome. The primroses would be distributed among a few closer friends or split into bowls around the house, where they would fleetingly delight the nose and the eye. Mother would smile, a little tearfully. Rather more often than the primroses, Mother's elder sister, Iris, would come up on a day excursion from London. Such an excursion cost ten shillings and sixpence, entailed four hours travelling in each direction, and enriched us with some six hours of her company. In these occasional visits Auntie Iris enlarged my life, bringing me books, answering my earliest questions, opening for me gradually over the years the world of ideas. Is it any wonder that I still remember her regularly in my prayers and count confidently on seeing her again, in God's good no-time?

My father's family were in Yorkshire, except for his sister, our Auntie Ethel, who lived only some ten minutes' walk away. My father was born and brought up in Yeoman Cottage, near Malham Cove. Only a few years ago I found the cottage and looked long at it and wondered at this link with so distant a past. The family were traditionally farm labourers but my father had chosen to break the pattern and to go to sea. Having been discharged from one of the more-prestigious lines as punishment for his political activities – he was known to address meetings on the Dock Road and was, I gather, a radical socialist – he was now working for Elder Dempster. This meant a series of tramp steamers, usually operating up and down the west coast of Africa; only when an occasional cargo brought them to a home port did he see his family and his family see him. I was ten when he died and missed him not at all, never having known him. Called into the army during what we once called the Great War, he met and married my mother, a Cornish village girl, carried her off and settled her in Liverpool – an unknown and unsuspected world. His family considered that he had married beneath him – even among the poor there are class distinctions – and my father's sister was soon not on speaking terms with my mother. This effectively and for long periods meant that we children were also cut off from this last possibility of family

8

ties. But we had surrogate grandparents. Our house was the last in the block and so possessed two huge rooms extending over the two corner shops beneath. It was larger than we needed and so, upstairs, lived the Calverts.

There were four Calverts: Arthur was groundsman for the Upton Cricket Club, over the water. We called him Gegga, an enduring memorial to our early attempts to pronounce Grandad. His wife, by a similar token Nanna, was almost as dear as my mother. There were two daughters, both at that time in their very early twenties. They worked in offices down town and related each evening anecdotes of the doings of their workmates, whom we soon knew by their nicknames though we never met them. There was no space for the Calverts to entertain visitors: how they all lived in two rooms was (or at least is now) a mystery. They were very much family and we loved them all, a link which endured until one by one they had all slipped away. Truly, in those days 93 Hall Lane was a cosy, enclosed, love-encrusted world.

Mother's friends in the neighbourhood were sometimes larger than life. One of her closest cronies was Win Noble, a massive woman, bespectacled, with a residual Irish accent, living in a tiny house built over some shops further down the road. Mr Noble was quiet, small, insignificant; he soon died and with his passing the world was in no way diminished. Win was the local uncertificated midwife, much in demand in the complex of pullulating back streets. Her recreations were two: jangling (the local term for feminine gossiping) and Guinness. I have, still, a vivid memory of her when Mother and I called on her one day: she was sitting at a table, surrounded by a zareba of empty bottles, candlelight glinting on her spectacles: the gas had once again been cut off in pursuance of arrears of payment. Win's hair was in considerable disarray and her capacious bosom was propped on the green tablecloth. (Why did women wear their lungs outside, I wondered?) She was singing, to herself until our arrival, 'Danny Boy', and as her voice rose for the 'oh Danny Boy' of the last line, it cracked and she dissolved into tears of boozy grief. Alcohol-

9

induced Weltschmerz,* I realise now, but at the time I gazed, unable to comprehend such massive sorrow. She had, I remember, legs like newell-posts and a habit of picking me up and crushing me to that pneumatic bosom, so that I had to fight to turn my head sideways that I might breathe.

My own birth, be it said, had been attended by the official midwife, Nurse Tamberlaine. I had been born with a caul, which the midwife kept as a great rarity, so that I had the comforting assurance that at least I should never drown. Indeed, my only doings with non-domestic water are in comfortingly-steady cross-Channel ferries, so that I have every confidence that the old sailors' superstition may in my own case be fully validated.

Win had two daughters, Shaddy and Madge. Shaddy was vivacious, enjoyed a busy social life and married a year or two later. Madge was rather withdrawn, had a cast in one eye, and early showed an unusual idiosyncracy: if she were in the street when any kind of a procession passed by, she would accompany the marchers, led by who knows what empathy. The Orange Lodges usually went no further than Netherfield Road, some two miles away, so represented no real danger. But the Foo-foo bands* came from outlying regions, out beyond Wavertree clock-tower, and Madge might be hours walking home. Boys' Brigade companies, Scout troops, even the British Union of Fascists or the Greenshirts, were likely to find that they had made an instantaneous and unwanted recruit. On May Day, indeed, Madge had to be confined to the house: the sight of gaily-bedecked horses was doubly entrancing and Madge might well end up in outer darkness, at Blundellsands or Formby or Prescot.

Just down the Lane was Mrs Tyson's grocery shop. It was decidedly, to use a modern term, down-market: low-ceilinged, dimly-lit, even in bright daylight. The floor was of bare boards on which was strewn a sprinkling of sawdust, changed weekly as a concession to hygiene. In front of the counter were several opened

* Commonly known as 'Boozers' Gloom'.
* Forerunners of the drum majorettes.

10

sacks, their tops turned over; from them Mrs Tyson used to scoop out salt or sugar or dried peas or some kind of grain; on top of the sacks slept the two cats, who had to be lifted off whenever access was desired. The shop smelt of household soap, disinfectant, cat urine and cheese, and was a notorious centre for jangling: once my mother got in there and other customers had drifted in to form a quorum, the session could go on for well over an hour. There is no flicker of doubt in my mind which is the more-communicative sex, and many later years of teaching teen-age children have only confirmed that early impression. If I had been trapped in there with Mum there was nothing for it but to give up hope of getting out for the immediate future and to stand, gazing out of the window, watching the passing traffic, thinking, nursing dreams of something better – real trees which you could climb, grass you might walk on, real rivers. Our only river, the Mersey, was so polluted and discoloured that if you had held some in a teaspoon you would not have been able to see the bottom of the bowl through the water. I half-listened to endless speculations: impending births, still births and miscarriages, terminal illnesses, suspicious associations. The spring welled endlessly. And who was this mysterious Sedon of whom they all spoke so frequently: 'When all Sedon done...?'

In consequence of unwilling attendance at many such sessions, it is still easy for me to reproduce such an occasion, all the more so as I have reason to believe that 'jangling' of this kind is by no means a lost art.

'I went up to make the boys' bed the other day. You know, the day we had all the rain. Wednesday, wasn't it? Or was it Tuesday? Well, anyway, I'd no sooner got on to the landing yes it was Wednesday I remember when I heard a regular tapping noise. I went round looking and there was a drip coming through the bathroom ceiling. One of those bleddy slates had shifted again. I keep telling that Mrs Fry about them but she never gets anything done. Well, I sent one of the boys for Mr Walmsley – Bob, I think it was: no, I tell a lie, it was Richard. He didn't get back for half an hour. Lives in a dream world, that boy. No sense of time at all.

11

D'you know, the other day he . . . Where was I? Oh yes. Well, Mr Walmsley came over and had a look and said he'd have to go back for a ladder. He looked real miserable. Never got over his wife dying like that and her not forty yet. Such a shame. Still, she wouldn't go and have it seen to, would she? Though we all told her. His daughter has given up her job and come to look after him. Didn't you know? Oh yes. Looks after him well but a bit of a madam. Only been home a month and already *getting very friendly* (quick nod of the head in my direction, acknowledged by corresponding nods from all the other women) with that Jack Fletcher in Costigans. And him a married man with two kids almost as old as she is. They're all talking about it. Of course, his wife doesn't *make him welcome* (more nods) so I suppose . . . Where was I? Oh yes. Mr Walmsley. Well I got a cup of tea ready for him and when I brought it in he wasn't there: gone, without a kiss-my-arse. He's like that, you know: on a bad day you can't get a word out of him. It's that Gladys Smith; she's got her hooks into him already. She always did fancy him, you know – oh yes. I used to see her looking at him in the shop. You could tell. Time she was married. Someone her own age, too. Anyway, after a time I sent one of the boys again to see when he was coming and there he was on the doorstep. And just then who should go past but that Ted Raynor. Have you seen him lately? His wife has been away for two months – looking after her mother, he says, but you never know, do you? He's getting very dressy. Flashy shirts and two-tone shoes: mutton dressed up as lamb, I can tell you. It's that young bit in the bread shop . . . She ought to know better. Anyway, he stopped to say hello – I wasn't very keen: I had plenty to do – and Mr Walmsley just ignored him. They used to be good mates. Funny how people can fall out about such little things, isn't it? I remember when it all started. That party at New Year. Nobody knows what the fight was really about but there they were on the parapet, going hammer and tongs. And then the night-sticks knocking on the pavement and the bobbies arriving from all directions. Where was I? Oh yes. Well, Mr Walmsley went up on the roof and he shouted down to me to hand him a hammer through the skylight. Just as I was going indoors to

12

find it that young bobby came past, you know, the one with the slight cast in one eye. The left, I think. Or is it the right? Such a nice chap. Only last week he...'

Eventually one of the other women would succeed in getting in a word or two, and this would be the thin end of the wedge: for the next five minutes or so, *she* would then monopolize the conversation and you could sense each of the others looking for the slightest crack through which she could creep, to have her two-pennyworth in her turn.

Yes, I am quite sure which is the more communicative sex.

Mum was friendly with all the local shopkeepers. With finances as precarious as ours, it was politic to be friendly, even if Mum had not been naturally so. Mr Piper managed Taylors' breadshop at the next corner; sleek, dark, thinning on top, he arrived very deliberately each morning on a cycle. It was he who once embarrassed me beyond measure when he caught me stealing biscuits, though he never told my mother. Ida, who managed Moorcroft's fruitshop and sold 'bruised' fruit at some incredibly-favourable price; Mr Walmsley, the chandler; the Allen family, opposite us, who made pickles and sauces (throughout my childhood I was rather fond of Lola, the daughter, with dark, come-hither eyes, smelling deliciously spicy); even the Chinese who ran the traditional laundry; and, of course, Mr Lennon who owned the pawnbroker's shop opposite 93. Every Monday morning showed a sad queue of women waiting to 'pop' various household articles for enough money to keep the family fed until the next pay-day – or the dole – came in: bedding, ornaments, china, a husband's Sunday suit (always worn either with a tie but no collar, or a collar with a large brass stud but no tie. To have worn both would have been over-ostentatious). There they would stand at the sign of the Three Brass Balls ('two to one you never get your goods back'), unwontedly subdued, willing perhaps to pop a wedding-ring – even in our street a sign of the greatest extremity of financial need. Some of the articles were later redeemed and some not, so that a pawnshop was an Aladdin's cave of every conceivable artefact. Pawnshops were essential parts of the economic system, recognised even in our songs:

> Mary Ellen at the pawn-shop door,
> A bundle in her hand and a bundle on the floor.

Once, I remember, a baby was handed-in, somehow rolled in an uninspected parcel of bedding. By the time somebody thought of going back to the pawnshop to look for it, the child was dead. We had shudders of delicious terror as we peered through the doorway into the dim interior and wondered aloud what other horrors might be concealed in its musty depths.

The front room was the only room of our house that did not show signs of over-occupation: the family foregathered there only on formal occasions – Christmas and the like – and the uniqueness of such occasions was heavily underlined by the fire burning in the blackleaded grate. There was a cheap leatherette (the very word betrays shoddiness) three-piece suite; a tall table in the window bay, on which stood an aspidistra; in one corner lurked a gas-meter, fed with frequent pennies once we had been adjudged too much of a security risk to merit being trusted with a quarterly account; there was a small, glass-fronted cupboard in which reposed a few trivial treasures which Mum had managed to hang on to: some hand-painted Japanese porcelain, a coy imitation-Dresden shepherdess and the like. Around the fire-grate were arranged a set of tools: a hearth-brush and long-handled shovel, a poker, fire-tongs. On the mantlepiece above stood 'me 'usbands vases' (pronounced as if spelt 'vawses'). There was, of course, the piano. In one corner stood a wickerwork table which creaked of itself: frightening in the twilight when I sneaked in alone for a dose of fear. The wallpaper showed a pattern of faded roses; there were a few pictures – 'And when did you last see your father?' will be with me until the day I die, so often did I stare at it and wonder what it was all about. I never asked. Long curtains partly hid the outside world but were ideal cover for furtive observation of everything that went on in the street. A session in the parlour was always enjoyed: we would all gather around the piano and sing quite unselfconsciously as Mum played; the brass candlesticks would shake and the faded scarlet rep behind the fretted woodwork would vibrate. Our tastes were catholic in the extreme: music-hall ballads of a bygone age:

> For I've got rings on my fingers, bells on my toes,
> Elephants to ride upon, my little Irish rose,
> So come be my neighbour and next Saint Patrick's Day
> Be Mistress Mumbo-jumbo Jittyboo Jay O'Shea.

Or our usual lullaby – and I could almost weep as I type the words:

> Go to sleep, my little piccaninny,
> Mother's going to smack you if you don't.
> Hushabye, rockabye, mammy's little baby,
> Mammy's little Alabama coon.

Sometimes Mother would sing to us as she played: 'Drifting and Dreaming', 'Golden Dreamboat', 'Songs of Araby'; does anyone at all still remember such songs, now? Sometimes, oddly, it was Moody and Sankey revivalist hymns – oddly, because Mother was bitterly hostile to all forms of organised religion. How the bitterness arose, I do not know, but it survived to her death; yet she exhibited all the dearer Christian virtues. So we gathered at the river with convincing heartiness. One of the familiar songs was an improving Victorian admonition from the pages of the *Strand Magazine*, one odd copy of which had been stranded on the improbable shore of 93, Hall Lane. Our version of it ended each stanza with the uplifting refrain. 'If at first you don't succeed, try, try again.' It was many years later that I discovered that the song was in fact a Württemberg folk-tune: 'Ach, wie ist's möglich dann . . .' There was, then, no wireless and we could not afford a gramophone, yet music played a part in our lives and the memory of those days is clearly etched into my mind. Many years later I found the scene perfectly painted for me by D H Lawrence:

15

'Softly, in the dusk, a woman is singing to me,
Taking me back down the vista of years till I see
A child sitting under the piano, in the boom of the tingling
    strings
And pressing the small, poised feet of a mother who smiles
    as she sings.
In spite of myself the imperious mastery of song
Betrays me back, until the heart of me weeps once again to
    belong
To the old Sunday evenings at home, with winter outside,
And hymns in the cosy parlour, the tinkling piano our
    guide.
So now it is vain for the singer to burst into clamour
At the great black piano appassionato; the glamour
Of childhood days is upon me. My manhood is cast
Down in a flood of remembrance. I weep like a child for
    the past.'

Yes, they were good, warm, comfortable, loving moments.

During most winters the pipes froze at one time or another, and sometimes during two periods in the same winter. Then we were not allowed a fire in the living-room: we were told darkly that the back-boiler would explode: another fear – my world was increasingly populated by fears and the worst were yet to come. The outside lavatory at the bottom of the yard would freeze, also; visits there were a torment, but somehow the cold-water pipe did not freeze and so we could always carry buckets of water around. The thaw would inevitably mean a drip somewhere and there would be much running about with basins and worrying talk about ceilings collapsing. At night I would lie in the gloom alongside my sleeping brother, staring into the invisibility above and imagining all that stained and cracked plaster falling swiftly and noiselessly to cover us. The regular split-splat of water into a waiting bucket was not reassuring.

The house was lit by gas though I can recall more than one occasion later when the gas had been cut off for non-payment of the bill. There was no shame in this: it was a local fact of life and at such times we would go over to candles for a few days until somehow the arrears were paid and the supply was restored. In the living and front rooms were gas mantles; all the other rooms had fish-tail jets which squealed incessantly and gave comparatively little light for the gas consumed. We usually went to bed by the light of a candle, carefully shielding the flame with a cupped palm in case the menacing darkness should extinguish it and leave us defenceless against unnamed terrors. Life, as I said, was full of fears. One that I still remember with some faint twinge of the old feeling was the weekly cleaning of the gas pipe in the middle room. Mum would climb on a chair, remove shade and mantle to expose the menacing pipe, then apply her mouth to the opening and blow. I always watched in apprehension: gas, I knew, was poisonous. The whole procedure seemed hazardous in the extreme. When Mum finally replaced mantle and shade and got down from the chair, there was always an exhalation of deep relief.

Not so dangerous but quite, quite nasty was the world of Nature, so far as it impinged on our home. If you went out into the scullery of an evening you would usually disturb the odd rituals of several cockroaches, performing who knows what incomprehensible rites on the cold tiles of the floor. Coming downstairs in the middle of the night, holding a flickering candle, treading gingerly with bare feet – you ran the very real risk of feeling and hearing a hideous, sickening crunching beneath your naked sole. Then occasionally we would realise that once again the bedroom had been invaded by bedbugs; their bites showed a different pattern from that of the ubiquitous flea. If you lit the candle you might well see a bloated bug crawling heavily up the wall, away from the scene of his feasting. You must not squash him: that would leave an incredibly-large bloodstain on the wallpaper. Standing the legs of the beds in small tins of paraffin availed only for a time: the things took to crawling across the ceiling and dropping accurately on to a sleeping form. Once we had recognised the current infestation, we would alert the Corporation; men would arrive and seal every aperture of the bedrooms, even caulking the door-frames. They would light

17

sulphur-candles and we would not be allowed back in for at least eight hours. This process left us free for a while but the horrible things inevitably returned eventually – the whole block was infested with them. Mice were another pest: in the quietness of a late evening as we sat reading, a small grey shape would move along the skirting-board towards the grate. Revulsion was very real and we would pursue the thing with pokers, boots and any other possible weapon. Usually, however, our unwelcome lodger would slip away through a crack: there were plenty of those.

Around now, with the prospect of school well over the horizon, my sister Betty was born. Win Noble practically took up residence; Mum had to take her to bed and Win fed Bob and me, washed and dressed us, prevented our occasional fights and shepherded us twice a day or so to see Mum. She assured us that Mum's illness would soon be over and breathed no word of the coming addition to our family. I was, in fact, over sixteen before I found out where babies came from: throughout my early teens it was a mystery which tantalised me intermittently. The age did not, as the present one, force sexual knowledge on children from an early age but did its successful best to hide such knowledge for as long as possible. One morning, then, we got up as usual, were shushed rather more vigorously than on other days, had breakfast and were enjoined to be good, that is quiet, because a marvellous surprise awaited us. So we sat there while mysterious errands went on all around – there seemed to be several neighbours in the house for no reason that we could see – then we were taken upstairs. And there we were introduced to the newest member of the family. Clearly, we were expected to be pleased: everyone else looked delighted – language seemed to have been abrogated in favour of incomprehensible cooing noises. It looked only half-finished, I thought; certainly Mum didn't look very strong. The newcomer could have picked a better time to join us, a time when Mum was her usual laughing, singing, vigorous self.

Then within a few months we were electrified to hear that we were all to go down to Cornwall for a week. Our grandparents were to us only a photograph and the regular weekly letter from Gran, identifiable by the crabbed angular fist on the envelope; what, we wondered, would the reality be like? One day, then, a taxi (a taxi!) drew up outside and in we all got. Mother, I knew, was as excited as we were: despite all her efforts she was quirking – the family name for Mum's perpetually-unsuccessful efforts to conceal a smile. At Lime Street we all found room in a train, in which we were to sit for no less than sixteen hours, and off we went. It must have been a trying journey but no memory of it survives. I recall only the large garden at the back of 4 Wood Lane, with real things really growing: magic! I picked up a windfall apple which had never seen, nor would ever see, a shop. Even at that age I knew vaguely that city life was cheating me of something I could neither name nor accurately describe. But I wanted to walk freely on untired grass, out of sight of railings and gravelled paths, to see and touch and smell. Too soon we were on the way back: when I stood in the front-room window, watching the rain bounce back from the flagstones, I could only imagine that each such spot was where a flower would grow if we removed all the pavements. Oddly, the Liverpool name for the pavement was the 'parapet': I wonder why.

Having arrived back, we were given two earth-shaking items of news: the Calverts were to leave us for a large house in Everton Valley, some miles away; and I was to start school. I had for long been reminded twice daily of my scholastic destiny: at ten to nine each weekday morning and at twenty past one each afternoon the school bell would ring. The school was only a hundred yards away and the sound of the bell, fixed in a kind of external belfry, carried clearly. Children, often in quite large groups each shepherded by an adult, would emerge from the surrounding streets and converge on the school. There were no school meals then: it was assumed that parents, not the State, would feed the children, and that break from school to the love and security of home in the middle of every day did much for the tone of schools and for the attitudes of children generally. Why, oh why, is so much Progress inevitably for the worse? The thought of school, then, did not worry me: my friends either went already, or would start with me, or would start before very long. The difficulty would be to adjust to the loss of the Calverts.

19

We were all sitting, I remember, in the Calverts' room one evening. There was a cheerful fire in the grate. I was sprawled on the carpet only a couple of feet away and the adults were sitting in a circle further back. Conversation came round to some mysterious character known as Da Ba* who chose, for inscrutable reasons, to live up the chimney. I expressed some scepticism and proof was offered. If I were to shut my eyes and ask Da Ba for something – say, the pair of gloves which I would need for the coming winter he would undoubtedly hear and respond. Less than half convinced, but knowing that I had nothing to lose, I performed the incantation and when, some seconds later, I opened my eyes, there on the carpet before me was a new pair of brown, woollen gloves. There was general astonishment, which I shared, at so speedy an answer to my request: clearly, Da Ba was a potent and benevolent being. I was permitted to shout my thanks up the chimney, this time without closing my eyes, and then it was bedtime. I am still pretty gullible, tending to accept at its face value whatever is said to me.

Then came school day. Dressed in the uniform of the time – high-neck jersey, short trousers, roll-top stockings and ankle boots – and with a handkerchief pinned ostentatiously to my left breast, I trotted off, hand in hand with Mum. The handkerchief was a vital part of any child's equipment: Liverpool's micro-climate was intensely favourable to the development of various respiratory diseases – of which the local pavements gave ample proof – and the local accent (then as now) was a unique blend of Welsh, Irish, ignorance and catarrh in equal measures. We joined a queue of similar couples, greeted the people we knew (Mum at once started jangling, quite forgetting me) and waited to be directed. Eventually, for the first time in my life I found myself being led away by a total stranger and glimpsed Mum only momentarily through the glass panel of a distant door – then even that sight was denied me. It was indeed a moment of truth. For some of the newcomers it was too, too much: there was some quiet snivelling

* Distantly related, they told me, to Icky the Fire Bobby.

and one boy, who turned out to be called Sammy Shakespeare, set up a prolonged bellowing which nobody could stop until fatigue intervened and transmuted it to a dispirited whine. The boy standing next to me, I was to know him later as Wedgewood Charles, looked imploringly at me – a look compounded of despair and an appeal for solidarity in this alien world.

Somehow the morning passed. We stood behind our hinged-top desks and greeted our new owner, Miss E A Pike. (We later learned illicitly, and gloried in the knowledge, that the initials stood for Edna Annie – the knowledge gave us some kind of hold over her). The Headmistress then handed us over to a class teacher who took us to another room and told us what we needed to know to be in the right place at the right time. At midday we were released to our waiting parents and whisked home for dinner, and a quick question-and-answer session, together with the injection of some moral boost, should that seem necessary. Then back to the playground: the caretaker, Mr Kitchen, in peaked cap, dark uniform and row of medal ribbons was now tugging rhythmically at the bell-rope for *me*. By now we knew enough to stand in a line when the handbell was rung and march in when desired; one last look round, half a wave, a tremulous smile and the huge jaws of the place had swallowed me again.

As the days passed, the routine became more than acceptable. I very quickly learned how to read and to recite my tables, was often picked to wash the leaves of the classroom aspidistras (a much-coveted chore) and less often to fill-in the daily weather-chart (a stylised sun or an umbrella or mist or even, later, snowflakes). Each day began and ended with a hymn and a prayer, and the last lesson of the day on Fridays was a play-session in the hall, during which an élite – of which I was not one – established a kind of proprietorial right over the coveted building bricks while rabbits like myself played board games or looked at illustrated books. Until now I had spoken a kind of neutral English: Mother's Cornish accent had faded though she had never acquired the local patois, Scouse. But now protective camouflage was necessary and I took to imitating the expressions of my classmates. It did not take

21

me long to develop two separate languages, one for use at home and the other for the playground. In recent years, surprisingly, the decidedly ugly and adenoid-inspired lingo of the Liverpool backstreets has become favoured of TV comedians: in those days we did not consider it funny. 'Ar ey, wack', spoken with considerable feeling, was a multi-use form of protest; 'yer wa?' did duty for 'I beg your pardon'; such phrases as 'Ayup, there's a scuffer up the jigger' warned of a policeman patrolling the alley behind the houses. An insult such as 'Bigged, got 'ned like Birkned', dared a fight, being answered with 'Yer wanna fight well, lah?' Many parents tried to eradicate the debased noises from the vocabulary of their offspring, but with only varied success.

My own social life moved from home to street, where even the simplest of resources sufficed to keep us contented: we rarely knew what it was to be bored – indeed, I doubt whether at the time I had even heard the word. Boredom is internal, not external: boring people are always bored, no matter what devices they may afford to adopt. We were so poor in material resources that we had to find interesting things to do and I took it for granted, then, that we should always succeed. A tennis ball could be used in a dozen different games; a length of rope transformed any lamp-post instantaneously into a swing or a maypole; there were droplets of congealed tar to pick out from between the cobblestones of the back streets and roll into a ball – which was then thrown away. This last contest always led to filthy hands and a subsequent inquest, often accompanied by tears – but we were always ready when someone again suggested such a contest a week later. In winter we would collect – carefully – the pile of red-hot ashes riddled from the firebox of a passing steam-lorry, put them into pierced tin cans and whirl the whole contraption round and round until flames came gushing out of every hole. These devices were known as winter-warmers, though most of the warming came of the exertion of twirling the thing vigorously round and round at the end of a piece of wire. When the declining days brought early dusk, distance was veiled attractively in mist: the paintings of Atkinson Grimshaw convey the atmosphere to the point of acute nostalgia.

The hard outlines were veiled; each street lamp had its aureole; distance was expunged. Then it was the time for wide games, variants of hide and seek, played over several acres of streets and back alleys. Imagination flourished, to our unheeded and unsuspected enrichment: how starved are the children of today with their wealth of toys and diversions which make no call on fantasy and thus convert eagerness into boredom into the lust for the next acquisition, all in an endless, expensive and unsatisfying chain. If all else failed, you could play guessing-games before the window of the sweetshop; none of us had much pocket-money and the child who could count on a regular 'Saturday penny' was held to be moderately fortunate. I had no regular income: on capricious and favoured occasions the manna of an unexpected penny would buy two ounces of sweets, or rather more in a 'home-mader', or even four ounces in one of the cut-price shops at the end of Botanic Road, at least twenty minutes' walk away. We thought nothing of that walk if it doubled the quantity of sweets to be gained from a windfall. Yes, life was full. Each evening started with a dash from the tea-table, the gang rallying cry – a yodelling and long-drawn-out 'Oo-ed', which would be answered by anyone within earshot (rather like a pack of wolves, it occurs to me now). Then the delights of that evening's spontaneities, terminated only reluctantly by distant shouts of 'Richard, you're wanted.' Such cries could be unheard for a time, but mounting adult frustration meant inevitably that the goodly fellowship must be dissolved for yet one more evening. My mother was never on speaking terms with the woman two doors away – between them existed a deep and abiding animosity – but her son Roy and I played together without any concessions to adult feuds.

The autumn term wore on, bringing a succession of local or national events, leading of course to the high spot of the school year: Christmas. The teachers earnestly explained to us deprived urban children the glories of harvest; we listened to word-pictures of golden corn and ripening fruit. Corn, we knew academically, had some distant relationship with bread – bread which was real once it came to us, wrapped in waxed-paper, from Taylor's. Some time around now, sliced bread was invented and at once found a ready market among hard-pressed mums. Fruit appeared in Moorcrofts, having been unloaded from a lorry. And before that? Even our imaginings did not reach so far. We were willing to accept that in theory trees were involved in the process at some stage, though careful inspection of the few discouraged trees in Kenny Gardens revealed no slightest trace of fruit.

One day, however, we all trotted off to school, bearing each an apple or an orange or perhaps a tin of cocoa powder. We were told that after the singing of some hymns – we ploughed the fields and scattered, whatever that meant – the various items would be given to needy children in local hospitals or orphanages. None of this had any practical relevance, of course, but then neither had anything else so earnestly retailed to us by dedicated teachers. It was all a great mystery and we had long ago learned to accept mysteries as part of the scheme of things: only home and the street were real and meaningful. Then came Teachers' Rest, a whole week in early October; for a short time the earlier freedom was restored, a week in which we could spend more time with Mum, or go out in daylight to play. Then Bobapple Night (gone, gone, alas), soon followed by Bonfire Night. It mattered not *why* Guy Fawkes wanted to blow up Parliament, whatever *that* was: what mattered was our bonfire and such fireworks as could be wheedled out of anyone with money and a kindly disposition. For weeks in advance we had been collecting anything inflammable and storing the hoard in a secure backyard (after all, some of it had come from others' hoards in insecure backyards). We had walked thrillingly, if illicitly, along countless backyard walls, looking down, assessing anything both combustible and portable. Even lavatory doors and seats were fair game, we thought. Local shops were pestered for unwanted boxes; the local joiner bestowed largesse of offcuts from various jobs, though more as a form of Danegeld than out of pure charity. On November 5th every side street was blocked, often in several places, by bonfires, each surrounded directly by excited children, at a decent remove by mothers – jangling, of course, while keeping a watchful eye on the doings of the younger children

– and even, further away, by small groups of men, sacrificing precious minutes en route to their clubs: the Warrington Arms, the Lord Derby or the Happy Union (not a married couple but a man and his dog). Sparklers would delight the smaller children; cannon-crashers would bang; rip-raps would cause localised panics, especially among the girls; rockets would soar into the sky, hob-nobbing there with alien rockets from other streets. In the darkness the flames created their savage beauty; the unheeded squalor was doubly disregarded. Slowly but all too quickly the night would wear on; the last fuel would be consumed and the flames would die down to a heap of glowing ash; the last visit to the shop would expend the last reluctant pennies; the last mothers would gather their satiated children, and Bonfire Night would be over for another year.

Then came the run-up to Christmas. For weeks in advance the classes had gone regularly into secret conclave, discussing how the room would be decorated and what kind of an item the class would offer in the school concert on the last day of term. Secrets were rapture: this year we would have icicles ('and you won't tell your friends in Class 4, will you?' As if we would). So we hacked about miles of crepe paper and made endless paper-chains. There were mobiles of all kinds to hang from the ceiling and a message of greeting, in enthusiastic if irregular capitals, to be affixed to the wall or window. Even a casual visitor to the school would have caught the throat-tightening rapture and expectancy of the time. A week before the great day our chatter was hardly to be restrained; in one conclave one little girl was so ecstatic that she wet herself, but this brought only sympathetic understanding, whereas at any other time it would have evoked scorn from the boys and fury from the other girls, who would resent this weapon so easily handed to their sworn enemies in the lifelong battle. And then, of all times, I was kept at home with some childish ailment.

It would be difficult to say which was more irksome: the physical symptoms or the knowledge of the delights that I was missing. On the way home from school my classmates would stand outside the window, as near as prudent parents would permit, and shout tidings of each day's doings, fragmentary and incoherent. At the party there would be cake. And Games. The Christmas tree was twenty feet high and the decorations . . . Each class now spent most of every afternoon preparing party turns, playlets, games. I ached to be well. Finally the great day came: the last day of term, the day of the Party. I knew the pangs of undiagnosed frustration as the afternoon bell clanged and my friends ran past, their faces alight with anticipation; as the last urgent footsteps died away I turned miserably back to the fire and my inadequate books. Even my mother could not console me. Just before four o'clock the children dashed past again, too excited to stop, wanting only to get home and recount the glories. They were wearing paper hats and carrying dishevelled parcels from which trailed coloured wrappings. And I had missed it all: there would never, I knew, be another Christmas. Then there was an imperious bang at the door knocker; my mother went to answer it and I heard her voice and another, unknown. Into the room came my mother followed by . . . no, yes, Edna Annie Pike. She had brought me treasure: a large and impressive paper hat (a bright-red fez, I remember), a packet of gaily-wrapped sweets and a mysterious parcel. The wrappings could not withstand my eager hands for more than a second or two, and there was a brightly-painted wooden boat with a sail and a rudder. How clearly I still remember that boat. And they had thought of me: I hope, now, that I conveyed my gratitude – though if I did, it was not in words. Then I left them (with Miss Pike one could hardly use the word) 'jangling', ran upstairs, part-filled the bath and launched my boat on its maiden voyage. It bobbed very convincingly on the ripples which I sent against it: most satisfying. For a few seconds I was parted from it, to hang over the banister rail and call a farewell to our visitor, then back to the boat. It did very little, true, except slide from one end of the bath to the other in obedience more to a thrusting finger than to frantic puffs directed at the tiny sail, but that little boat was the final extension of a strong imagination. That was one thing of which we were never short: imagination. Outside in the street, any one of us could transform himself immediately into a mighty locomotive, bent forearms

26

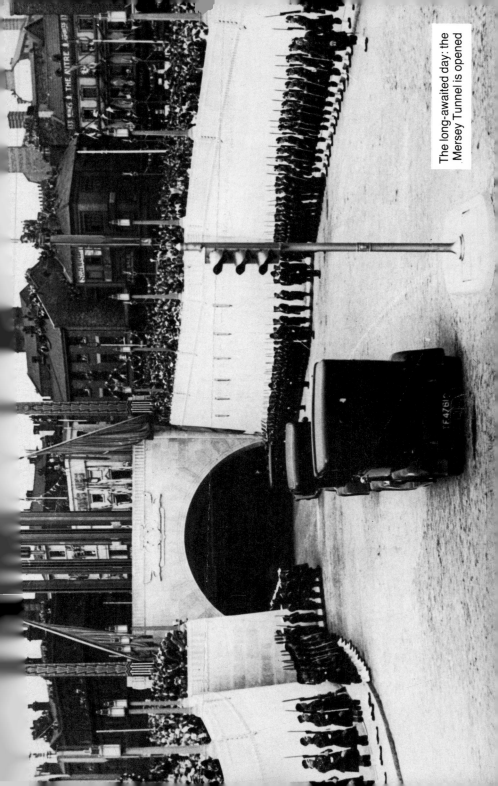

The long-awaited day: the
Mersey Tunnel is opened

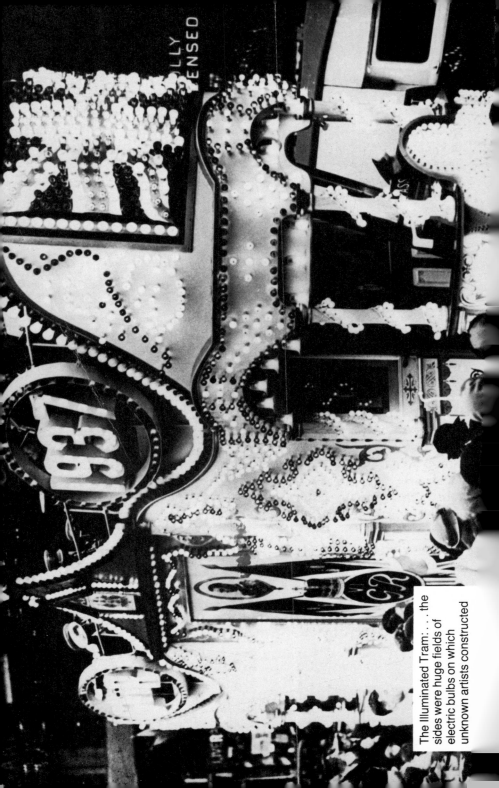

The Illuminated Tram: . . . the sides were huge fields of electric bulbs on which unknown artists constructed

imitating conrods, the puffing of infant breath sufficing for the snorting of those massive cylinders. Or we would be a multiplicity of Tom Mixes, galloping across the Liverpool prairie, each of us rider and steed combined centaur-like. Or some hero of the moment: Dixie Deans or Elisha Scott or Patsy Hendren or Harold Larwood. There were giants in those days, indeed. If confined to the house by lowering skies and unwanted rain, I could transform at will the legs of an easel, of which the blackboard had long splintered into disuse, into the sixteen-inch guns of a warship, and an upturned table would represent the ship itself. Or a life-raft, bobbing on a limitless ocean. Faithful and patient old Bonzo would, unknowingly, be transformed to a lion – though attempts to explain to him the role required or even to stalk him, as a big-game hunter would approach his intended prey, produced only canine confusion, a downturned tail, a short whine of despair and a swift retreat.

So life went on. School on weekdays; on Saturdays shopping with Mum – always a burden, this, because Mum could be confidently expected to meet at least two bosom friends every hundred yards and each such meeting automatically began a jangling session which might go on endlessly. Watching the passing traffic soon palled: delivery vans, the bread cart (the bread boy, Jim, was a close friend), steam lorries, each with a stoker sitting alongside the driver and stooping occasionally to shovel more coke into the mini-furnace which produced the driving force. An occasional charabanc, a motor-cycle with sidecar, an infrequent private car ('You can have any colour you like,' said Henry Ford, 'as long as it's black'). A policeman might cycle purposefully past, missing nothing on his patch. He knew each of us children and our parents and was inclined to settle the bill for minor peccadillos among the children with the flat of one large hand applied where it would cause the maximum of healthy reflection. Such summary punishment was kept secret from parents, who could confidently be counted upon to double the dose just to make sure that the lesson had sunk in. Very, very occasionally there would be an unmistakeable noise. All conversations would stop, cyclists would dismount, faces would turn upward and soon many pointing fingers would indicate the aeroplane creeping across our sky. Only when it had vanished over the rooftops would life continue. Some day, I resolved (at the age of seven or so) some day I, too, would fly.

Horse-drawn carts were so common as not to merit a look; the signs of their passing were unheeded – in our area there were no gardeners whatever. Milkman's traps were invariably drawn by failed race-horses. The milkman would stop, remove the lid of a brightly-polished churn, dip in the appropriate measure and decant the milk either directly into a proffered jug or into an aluminium can, which would then be left on the doorstep. Our local milkman, for whom I would later work, was Ernie Walker. The dairy was a few yards away from 93. He was tall and lean, raw-boned and red-faced: my mother was wont to say of him, 'His face is like a farmer's arse on a frosty morning.' My mother's language was a cause of perpetual embarrassment to me: I was a prissy child (and it was to be another ten years before the Royal Air Force cured me of that). Ernie was married to a wife, Jay, of cultural pretensions. She never ceased to deplore that her life had to be lived out in such a cultural jungle: Ernie hardly came up to her requirements. Coalmen, always in twos, would drive their flat carts up and down the sidestreets, slumped on the seat, in wet weather covered with the ubiquitous slit-open tarred sacks which did duty for souwester and mac alike. The clip-clopping of the horses' hooves on the cobbles and the repetitious, lugubrious, long-drawn-out shout of 'Coal' – these noises were the background to our lives. Coal was one-and-eight a hundredweight, I remember, in an age when an unskilled clerk or labourer, if he could find work at all, would be paid two pounds five shillings a week. There was, incredibly, no inflation whatever then: prices were fixed by immutable law. A twopenny bar of chocolate remained a twopenny bar of chocolate from the time when I was born to some time during the last war; a threeha'penny stamp would take a letter from one end of the country to another – and if it had been posted before eight in the evening, could be counted upon to arrive by a morning delivery the following day. A local letter posted before eleven a.m. would be delivered by four the same day. Who prates of progress? And all this was done without any of the expensive aids without which the Post Office simply could not function in these days.

During those early years, then, life was comfortingly secure. Each morning I would be awoken and bidden to wash. Sometimes I would find, on waking, that I could not open my eyes: some childish ailment would have gummed the lashes together. A panic-stricken wail would bring a comforting presence, a soothing voice, the promise of immediate relief, and a bowl of warm water which soon put things right. Then I would be placed before a bowl of porridge – 'burgoo' in the family – on whose sickening grey surface would be sprinkled sugar and over all milk would be poured. I would be sternly bidden to eat this revolting glop until Tom, Tom the Piper's Son showed up clearly from the bottom of the dish. Not long ago I presented that same dish to an honorary godson, who lost no time in breaking it. Historical relic or not, serve it right. There were days when no combination of threats, bribery, cajolery or pleading would suffice and then I would be force-fed.* One day, I remember, I was adjudged to be so ill that I need not get up: breakfast would be brought to me in bed. When the porridge arrived, there were lumps in it: doubly disgusting. Yet when Mother came upstairs soon afterwards, quite prepared for the usual struggle, I was lying back on my pillows and Tom, Tom was plain for all the world to see. I was praised and rewarded with an extra piece of fried bread. It was not until the following day that my mother discovered the porridge, thrown in desperation all over the back of the dressing-table. The reckoning was formidable: I remember it still.

I enjoyed school despite its purely-academic character: between life inside the school and outside there was no correlation whatever. I was simultaneously a citizen of two utterly-unrelated worlds. The pictures so lovingly pinned-up for us were incomprehensible, as were the songs we sang.

---

* Porridge was held to 'put a skin on your belly like velvet'.

Come with me, come with me,
Through the old gate by the apple-tree.
Oh, what wondrous sights you'll see
Down where the blossom's blowing.

There was a picture of what I now know to be an orchard in full blossom: it was so alien to mucky, sordid, unbeautiful, *horrible* Liverpool that the words conveyed only a semantic blank and the picture was mentally filed under 'fairy-tales'. Twenty years later I did, for the first time ever, see trees in blossom: following a series of operations I was allowed out of hospital for the day; I emerged from the front gate of the RAF station at Uxbridge and was met by the sight of the wild cherry trees in the garden of Saint Andrew's church opposite, in full glorious blossom. For me, the sight was breathtaking. I could only stand and worship,* conscious of wonder and gratitude and reverence, the ingredients of all true worship. Even now I am likely to walk round and round a tree in blossom, renewing the wonder. But at least school taught me to read: a gift which has been of such value that the words themselves are just silly. By the time I was seven I could read fluently and every day included a visit to the local library, some ten minutes' walk away. I would dash home from school, pick up yesterday's expended book and run to the library. Then the agonised choice – we were allowed only one book at a time – and the slow saunter home for tea, reading as I ambled. I often collided with lampposts which brought me instantaneously back from a private world into the everyday. Saturday's book was, of course, finished long before the day was over and Sunday was a desert. Soon I discovered that most of the neighbours had small private libraries, so I read my way through these, too. If all else failed I would re-read, for the umpteenth time, the books which we had at home: 'The Cruise of the Rattler' (Ballantyne, I think); 'Tom Brown's Schooldays'; 'The First Men in the Moon' (ridiculous: whatever next?); 'Tales of the Ring and Camp' and 'The Exploits of Brigadier Gerard', both by

---

* Should I put off the shoes from off my feet?

Conan Doyle; 'Little Women and Good Wives' (I had no notion that it was a *girl's* book: a book was a book was a book); some Henty, Jack London, Marryatt. 'The Man in the Iron Mask' remained beyond me and there were none by my favourite author, Percy F Westerman. As I said, most houses had books and, in memory, most people had read their books. So different from our own enlightened age.

About now a Mrs Feinburgh, who lived at the top of Tillotson Street, took to calling on Sunday afternoons and whisking me off to St Mary's Sunday School. This was held in the huge, bare barn of the Church Hall; we sat in little groups, each around a teacher, had a short Bible lesson, were given text-cards (each with a fascinating coloured picture of New Testament days) and then coalesced for a short and simple service. Afterwards Mrs F would gather her flock and deliver them all to their rightful owners. From Mother's point of view it was simply one third of her brood off her hands for an hour or more each Sunday afternoon; from my own, it was the necessary run-up to the annual Treat. One day we all climbed into a couple of charabancs, were driven off to Sefton Park and organised into games on the grass there, followed by what were then called light refreshments. Quite soon after the Treat I declined to attend Sunday School any more: the investment, I thought, was not worth the dividend. So ended my first brush with organised religion, but my next was not long in coming. On Thursday of each week Mother would stoke up the fire under the huge copper boiler in the scullery and it was wash-day again. The place would fill with steam; the clothes would be boiled and removed for a session in the tub with the dolly-pegs, primitive and man-powered fore-runners of a modern washing machine. In a few things at least progress has been for the good. Then the mangle, which creaked and ground as floods of water were pressed out, followed by hanging on the line in the yard, if the weather was right, or over the 'pulley' fixed to the ceiling if must be. To assist her, Mother could afford the few pence to reward Mrs Killen. Mrs K came from a tiny house somewhere off Bowler Street – even by our standards a poor area – was a childless widow and lived alone.

She had, I remember, but one tooth – one. This was in the middle front of her upper jaw and obviously of no practical assistance in eating: I presume now that she lived on soft foods. The mainspring of her life was her membership of the Salvation Army. As she went about her work she would carol:

> I've got the joy, joy, joy, joy,
> Down in my heart, down in my heart, down in my heart.
> I've got the joy, joy, joy, joy,
> Down in my heart –
> Glory to His name.

I can hear her singing still, even as I write. One Sunday she called for me, resplendent in bonnet and some kind of uniform – I remember only the bonnet – and took me to the Citadel. It was brightly lit by many gas-mantles, and although we arrived quite twenty minutes before the service was due to begin, there was a lot of singing going on. On a platform was a band, similar to the one which sometimes played in the park on Sunday evenings in summer. Everybody, it seemed, was wearing uniform and singing with great fervour. At least I knew *one* of the choruses, and piped up with it, but for the rest I understood little. The service seemed to go on for a very long time and it was quite bedtime before we got home. I never asked to go again, but Somebody clearly had plans for me for a third encounter, a few years later, turned out to be very final, as will appear. Mother was not at all surprised that neither of my two brushes with religion had 'taken' – she had expected nothing else.

With the passing of the days my consciousness expanded: I came to see our neighbours in the block as the inhabitants of a village and felt the beginnings of a community sense. At the far end and living next to and over the breadshop were Dorothy's family; as I grew older, I found, I no longer had to share my bath with Dorothy. I did not know why and did not ask: I was just relieved to be alone in there. Next door lived Mrs Coffee, short, dumpy, yellow of skin, living alone and rarely seen. Then the Harrison family, with twin boys a year or two older than myself; somehow, they never joined our loose and informal gang. Then the Hodgkins family, all grown-up, and, sharing their doorstep, the Rieglers, Mr and Mrs. They were Germans and had come to live in the Lane quite soon after the war. Their first night there was evidently the first night of their marriage: through the thin lath and plaster wall between the bedrooms Mrs Riegler was clearly heard to implore, 'No, not like that. You'll tear it. Look, there's a button here.' Zip fasteners were still waiting to be invented. Then came the Jones family – Welsh-speaking at home: incomprehensible. The daughter, Marjorie, suffered from some kind of fits; she lived all day in a semi-upright pram, made inarticulate noises and if excited thrashed about with her arms and legs, emitting anguished cries. The son, Willie, once took me to a social evening at their chapel: the programme consisted of choral items, piano pieces, narrative items and hymns in unison. Both these latter were in Welsh, so I could join in neither the singing nor the laughter. Next door to them were the Christians; Roy was my frequent companion, but his mother and mine, as I have said, were sworn enemies. Some years later that enmity was to result in a public fracas, as a result of which both women were bound over to keep the peace, the magistrate having failed to make sense of their charges and counter-charges. Mr Christian was a motor mechanic and was reputed to store petrol in the small shed which he had built at the bottom of his yard. Jangling speculations about the likely consequences of a fire added another possible fear to my nocturnal imaginings (although the worst by far was still to come). The daughter, another Marjory, was a couple of years older than myself, sweet-natured and, it seemed, repressed at home. She later caused great scandal by running away and finding relatives somewhere in wildest Lancashire. Sharing our doorstep was Mrs Marr, tall, ladylike, reserved but quietly friendly. We did not see much of her and it seems to me now that she might have been away a great deal. On the other side of us and forming the corner with Albany Road were two shops. One of them was used by Mr Cobb, a jobbing carpenter, and the other by Mr Moore, a shoe-repairer. The latter shop was significant. The machine on which he finished-off the repairs was driven by an electric motor, and when occasionally Mother was out in the evening I would lie in the darkness overhead, conscious of my responsibility for my brother and sister, and hear the machine start up as he worked overtime to get the jobs ready for the following day. The sound was inexplicably menacing, like the rumbling roar of some far-off and approaching monster. What a relief when I heard the front door slam and the voice of Mum in the hall. I never revealed to her that fear, I do not know why.

That, then, was our block. Awareness attenuated as one probed ever further in this direction or that. Towards Kenny Gardens the streets were laid out uniformly; the houses were well-painted, with daily-scrubbed doorsteps, the edges finished in contrasting red. The first sign of a good housewife was her doorstep, and if you were too ill to perform the ritual cleaning, it was the first job a friendly neighbour would do that your reputation might be maintained. The streets leading down from the other side of the Lane were slummy, despised, full of snotty-nosed infants and gangs of unshod boys their bare feet slapping on the paving stones. In the afternoons, women would sit on their front door-sills and exchange gossip across the narrow streets. At the very bottom of Bengel Street was the ultimate in degradation: Back Mount Vernon View. Dickens would have recognised it immediately. It was a short cul-de-sac of wretched hovels, where front doors opened directly into living-rooms. Two up and two down, they were; several houses shared a lavatory and an adjacent standpipe. There was usually a younger child squatting like an animal in the gutter, oblivious of the public gaze. However poor, however desperate, we later became, at least we never sank to that level. We often, later, had to huddle silently at the back of the house until the landlady gave up her attempt to collect the fifteen shillings rent, to say nothing of the arrears. I do not remember how we cooked on the not infrequent occasions when the gas was cut off. I recall many days when I went to school with holes in the soles of my shoes – walking around the puddles alleviated the discomfort – but at least

34

I never went unshod. How did the barefooted boys cope in the frost, I wonder now. And a half-empty belly gave no outward sign. Looking back, I realise now that my later school career was stunted not only by innate laziness but also by undernourishment: there is not much food value for a growing boy in stale buns and bruised apples, jam butties, salt fish, and meat only on Sundays and occasional high days. Sunday dinner was invariably 'dry hash': a tin of corned beef* beaten into mashed potato and fried, served with marrowfat peas which had been soaked throughout the night and then boiled. Plus, to give that touch of damn-the-expense-give-the-cat-another-goldfish, a bottle of Tizer between us. I wish, now, I had looked to see how much my mother awarded herself. No wonder that we were all unquestioningly and utterly Labour; our hero (or do I mean heroine?) was Mrs Braddock and our anthem the Red Flag.

> So raise the scarlet banner high:
> Shout revolution to the sky.
> Though cowards flinch and traitors sneer,
> We'll keep the red flag flying here.

Good, stirring stuff: more hopes ripe for later betrayal when it turned out that the working class, given power, was no more noble than the capitalist, no more given to handing out freedom for all, no less motivated by self interest. It took me most of a lifetime to see that the cause of all our ills lies in the very nature of man. 'There was never any thing by the wit of man so well devised nor so sure established which, in continuance of time, hath not been corrupted,' states the introduction to the Prayer-Book, with clearer view than any political idealist. I remember still, with a pale shadow of the original shudder, the day when I took the family's last sixpence down to Ellis's for the usual weekend tin of corned beef. While I was waiting to be served, the coin slipped from my fingers, rolled across the bare boards of the floor and before my

---

* Known to the family as 'bullamacow'.

horrified eyes slipped down a crack and was gone. The shock was too great for any expression: 'I tell you, hopeless grief is passionless, That only men incredulous of despair... Beat upwards to God's throne in loud access Of shrieking and reproach.' Something of this must have shown on my face for Mr Ellis came around from his side of the counter, laid a hand comfortingly on my shoulder and presented me with a tin. Some of the damned in Hell have been granted an annual day out on an iceberg for less, it has been said. I went home in dazed relief and have said nothing of it to this day.

However, those days were still ahead. At the age of six I found life tolerably secure. My father was away somewhere on a ship and money arrived from him, via the shipping office, each week. I was happy and secure at the Rathbone School, where my brother Bob would join me in the following autumn. Our sister Betty was idolised by us all, a living doll, and her schooling lay several years ahead. And always there was Mother, the lynch-pin of the family. In the evenings, after the ritual and painful haircombing, with a fine-toothed comb ('Look. There's another of them') we would play hunt the thimble or board games, or we would sing around the piano; 'Ten men went to mow' was always popular. Or I would read and my mother would get out her mending while the other two busied themselves with something or other: once I was immersed in a book I knew little of what else was going on around me.

It was just before my second Christmas at school that the first turning-point came, the beginning of a nightmare that was only to intensify over the next eight years. It began so harmlessly. For months I had been paying-in to the school bank to ensure that there would be something extra for Christmas. By the end of term the princely sum of twenty-five shillings had been deposited. All that fabulous richness was earmarked for food or toys or whatever else was needed to give the expected glow to the time. On the very last afternoon of term Miss Pike came into the room and said – and to this day I swear that this is what she said – 'All those girls who want to withdraw money from the bank, come to my room now.' I was very literal-minded (indeed, I am still) and sat tight, waiting for the boys to be called. They weren't, and I went home at the end of the day without the money. When I told mother she was too stunned even to be angry: she had counted so absolutely on that money and in its absence could see no possible way ahead. She sat silently in her chair, looking at me. I suddenly realised that something indescribably tragic had happened: I cried out – and I remember the anguish still – 'Oh Mummy, are we *poor?*'

I do not remember how we coped that Christmas: only the one moment is as clear in recollection now as it was then. Such sums were not to be borrowed from our friends, however willing: local budgets did not even stretch from week-end to week-end, hence the need for the pawnshop. Perhaps that is how Mother solved the immediate difficulty then: I do not know. But from that afternoon I count the start of the bad days, though they came, at first, only slowly. The catastrophic decline in our fortunes was still a year or two ahead.

2

'It's a wise child that...'

Some time around now, then, came a change in the pattern and quality of our lives. One afternoon there was a knock at the front door; At the age of, perhaps, seven I was minding the house and my siblings; my mother was, I knew, jangling in the Jones house, three doors away. I went to the door and opened it; on the step was a strange man. He looked at me almost expectantly.

'Yes?' I queried.

There was a short pause before he answered, 'Is your mother in?'

'Just a moment,' I replied. 'I'll fetch her.'

I left him on the step, shut the door, went back through the house and out by the back door, and down the entry to Jones's.

'Mum,' I reported. 'There's a man at the door, asking for you.'

'Who is it?' she asked, cut off in mid-sentence.

'I don't know,' I replied helplessly. 'He just wants to speak to you.'

'All right. I'll come now.'

I went back home and within a few minutes she came in at the back and went through the house; I heard her opening the front door. I heard an exclamation and two voices. Soon she came back into the room, the stranger behind her. She looked at me scornfully.

'You bloody fool,' she said. 'That's your father.'

Really? I looked at him: tall but rather stooped, sallow, rather hook-nosed, utterly unknown. He must indeed have been my

38

father: all the evidence pointed that way. He sat, as of right, in Daddy's chair; usually a doting Bonzo sat either at his feet or on his lap; He slept in Mum's bedroom; he had the key of the door, though he rarely went out; he sat with us at meals. For him I had no flicker of feeling whatever: he might have been a mobile article of furniture. Clearly, he was now out of a job. Soon there was talk of Quebec, or was it Montreal?, and he vanished again. If all went well in Canada (Canada? Where was that?) we would all move out there and join him; he was now, apparently, a chef in a hotel. But at the end of the holiday season he was home again. Within a month or two he went off to work in another hotel, this time in Keswick, but with the end of the season he was again back home. Still, it did mean that we all went up to Keswick for a week's holiday, the second in my young life. We lived in rooms with the Graves family. For a glorious few days we were free of an enchanting countryside: we climbed the lower slopes of Skiddaw. There was honeysuckle; there were foxgloves; there were no gravel paths or railings; the terrain was uneven, often enclosed by trees. When we awoke of a morning the mountain beckoned against a blue sky. A trip around Derwentwater in a huge launch was sheer ecstasy, not to be marred by mere conversation. Every detail was filed away for later regurgitation: the surrounding hills; the unsullied light; the clean and glassy water; the absence of land, streets, traffic. The whole week was ecstasy but at least when we all returned to Liverpool I carried back the memory of what I had always longed for and suspected was there for the finding: the untarnished wonder of a free countryside. Two memories persisted: there was a suspension bridge and if we all jumped up and down the structure would vibrate faintly under our feet; and there was a very real witch. At the time I was suffering quite badly with several warts on my hands – chiefly, I remember, the right hand. The strongly-Salvationist Mrs Graves told mother of the address and powers of this old lady and off we went. I remember an old cottage, much in need of paint, and an overgrown garden and dirty windows. The fence and gate badly needed repair. We walked up the front path and knocked at the door; I was merely curious but, I think now, my mother was apprehensive. The witch, small, wrinkled and yellow of skin, listened to my mother – who seemed, inexplicably, to be in less than full command of the situation – then told us to sit down and went out into the garden. Through the filthy curtains we saw her stooping occasionally and plucking various plants, though when she came back the only kind I recognised were the dandelions. These were known to us as pee-the-beds, a name which guaranteed that under no circumstances would we ever pick them, and I felt a vague concern for my own nocturnal comfort. She crushed all the plants in her hands, rolling them between her palms, her lips moving inaudibly. Then she bade me hold out my hands and she rubbed the fibrous, juicy mixture over all my warts. Now I could hear her mumbling, though I could not hear clearly what she was saying. Finally I was ordered under no circumstances to wash my hands until the following day – would that all prescriptions were as welcome – and we left. Mother trailed behind so that she could discuss last-minute affairs. We went down to the open ground beside the lake: the wooden stands for the Keswick Convention were already in place and we climbed all over them, enjoying the changed viewpoint. I do not remember that we discussed the exorcism or even that I thought about it again that day: throughout that week I lived not only in the moment but with all my attention focussed sharply on each passing milli-second. I knew that everything, but everything, was to be stored away in the greatest detail for later use.

On the following morning it was not until I came to wash that I remembered my warts and realised that they had all vanished, leaving no trace behind. I was not particularly impressed, I recall: that was precisely what witches were for; nor do I recall any family discussion: the whole thing was over. But for a second or two the relief was enormous.

All the following winter my father was out of work again but with the early spring off he went to yet another hotel, this time in Whitby. At the end of the season he came back. There was no work the following season or ever again. I remember that that Christmas we had to accept a parcel from the Goodfellows: chicken, cake, pudding, butter, tea, various tins and packets. I remember my father staring at it all as my mother unpacked it. We children knew not the word charity; we saw only the fact and cared not whence the food came. But when I went out into the scullery, later, my father was there, leaning with his face against the roller-towel which hung behind the door, weeping. The sight was so terrible that I could not move: for me, as for Job, the earth was shaken out of her place and the pillars thereof trembled. I said nothing; I do not know whether he remarked my presence. I went back into the other room, picked up my book, tried to read, despite the shock which was still powerfully with me. It was many, many years before I understood the overpowering shame and grief of an honest man unable by his labours to provide for the needs of his family. My father never worked again. These attempts to find a job ashore, I now realise, so that he might find more time to be with his family, had failed and by now the deepening slump had cut heavily the jobs available at sea. Liverpool was full of sailors 'on the beach': they leaned against walls the length of Goree or the Dock Road, never too far from a pub, just in case. They sat around on the Landing Stage, eyeing the diminished number of ships in the river, spitting moodily into the murky water. They thronged the premises of the Mersey Mission to Seamen. It was a time of widespread hopelessness, of desperate women and hungry children. Our lives were no different from many others.

Soon my father took to his bed; some tropical disease, picked up on the west coast of Africa, my mother said. Mum went up and down with trays of food and often when she came down again there were tears on her face. I do not recall that we children ever went in to see him, as we did not visit him later when he was admitted to Mill Road Hospital. Then I was awakened in the early hours of one morning; for some reason which I do not recall, I was sleeping in the front room, on a bed which had been brought downstairs. Mother was bending over me; half awake and half asleep, I knew at least that she was real, but that surely couldn't be a policeman behind her? She told me that she had to go to the hospital and that I had to listen in case either of the other two awoke. When I next

41

awoke, at the usual time, Mother was drawing down the blinds of the windows; she was crying. She told me that my father was dead, which produced no flicker of feeling of any kind. Later I went off to school carrying a note to my class teacher, Miss Qualtrough, of whom I was inordinately fond. Throughout the day I harvested, uncomprehending, an unexpected crop of sympathetic looks and soothing pats on the head. It was all utterly meaningless. I was almost ten years old and it is only now, more than half a century later, that I have some dim idea of what I may have lost that day. Some idea, too, of what he may have lost: a wife he rarely saw and a family who hardly belonged to him. Oddly, apart from Mother, the only other that I remember to have shown signs of loss was Bonzo: he would wander in from the scullery, go over to my father's chair as so often before, look up at where a head would have been, whine imploringly and wag his stumpy tail propitiatingly, then lower head and tail and settle down on the carpet. Quite clearly, he was communicating with someone whom he could see though we could not. Yet it was years before any of us could bring ourselves to sit in Daddy's chair.

Looking back now, I can sum up all my experience of my father in three unrelated episodes: they seem to have left significant memories – even scars, perhaps?

When I was perhaps eight or nine years old, he and I went off one day to a football match, to see Liverpool play against Everton. It was my first visit to such an occasion (and it was to be another forty years before I went again) and I stared around with considerable interest. We were standing quite a long way up and away from the arena and surrounded by a dense crowd, almost exclusively men. Most of them were smoking and a dense blue cloud hung over us. It was very noisy: there was some disorganised and preliminary chanting, a few individual voices raised in raucous song, sporadic attempts to start the chorus of an obvious anthem: 'Ay, aye, we'll win the match.' I could not see what all this racket had to do with a football match: football, I knew, was a game which we played when we couldn't think of anything more immediately attractive to do. After a time the players appeared in that distant amphitheatre, flickering and multicoloured pygmies on the muddy-green grass. A whistle shrilled and play started. At once the spectators showed all the signs of hysteria: grown men were yelling hoarsely, jumping intermittently into the air, maligning the referee. The noise was an indescribable resultant of song, curses and incoherent expressions of some overpowering emotion. I realised that the stranger beside me, even, was shouting and occasionally waving his arms. I was mute: there was no reason that I could see for this massive expenditure of emotion: just a football game going on down there. It was all beyond reason. From time to time my father broke off in his ravings and looked down at me and our eyes met. He would shake his head sadly then redirect his attention to the game. At half-time he left me for, I knew, neckoil (a composite word which I never associated with its component parts), and reappeared in fierce argument with a stranger.

At last the match ended; I forget, now, who won – the result is as important to me now as it was then. Ludo, draughts, football, snakes and ladders – all just games, surely, which you played for half an hour's diversion and then forgot as the next diversion offered itself. On the long walk home my father tried unsuccessfully to discuss with me some points of the game but he soon realised that I had not seen the play, having been more interested in the antics of the spectators – especially one or two incipient fights which, alas, came to nothing. My father (the very phrase sounds passing strange) never tried again to interest me in football.

Memory two. I came home one day, crying. Questioned, I revealed that I had had a fight with Roy Christian, which I had lost. My brother was sent to find Roy, who soon arrived in a mixture of truculence and trepidation. To his considerable surprise, he was presented with sixpence – riches, to us. I could not remember my father ever having given *me* sixpence. The intention, clearly was to needle me into winning my fights, but once word got around, the result was entirely predictable: the neighbourhood buckos practically queued up to get at me. I hardly dared go out in daylight. Once a week or so, despite all my precautions, my father paid out the by now customary sixpence. Then one day I had had enough. The current tormentor had interrupted a game of rounders and I seized the bat and lashed out at him. I intended to hit him across the side of the head but my vicious swing missed and hit him across the neck. He burst into tears and turned to run away, in the course of which I caught him most satisfyingly across the back of the head; after that I could not catch him, though I tried, running as fast as I could after him, calling out whatever curses I knew. Had I caught him, I might well have killed him, or at least injured him severely. Then, and only then, did I burst into tears: the relief of nervous tension, I expect. Drying my eyes and accepting the congratulations of my friends, I eventually set off home, already spending the sixpence which I had surely earned. But by the time that I got there, my victim and his mother were also arriving. There was an immediate post mortem; although I explained that I had not started the fracas, it availed nothing. For some reason which I did not understand, my father was again furious with me. I was sent to bed in mute disgrace. The reasoning still escapes me: when, later, I was called to fight in my country's quarrel, I was given a bombing aircraft and a machine-gun to do it with. Eminently sensible. In later years, as a schoolmaster, I counselled many unaggressive boys: do everything in your power to avoid a fight, but if a fight is forced on you, pick up the nearest blunt instrument and lay about you. Someone will always pull you off before you can inflict major harm, and if there *is* an inquest, you can always plead self-defence. On several occasions over the years, my advice was taken and in each case the intended effect was achieved: the bullying stopped, word having got around that it didn't pay.

It was plain to me that my father was disappointed, holding me to be an unmanly son: but the bullying stopped.

My third and final memory is also less than happy. In my last two years at the Elementary School I was selected as potential scholarship material and used to come home with homework in English and Arithmetic; the English was easy enough – a joy to do, in fact – but the maths caused much struggling and even the occasional tear of frustration. My father would read the current

44

conundrums over my shoulder, do the whole lot in his head, sigh with a mixture of contempt and disappointment, write down the answers on a slip of paper and then put the paper ostentatiously under a vase which stood at the end of the mantlepiece. When, somehow, I had finished the exercise, at least half a troubled hour later, he would take down the piece of paper, show me that he had so quickly and easily got the same answers, sigh again and leave me to pack my books away. I could not escape the knowledge of my own stupidity.

Yes, on all accounts, I see that I must have been a great disappointment to him.

Life, then, was predominantly school, the street and home. I did well in school: it was small and personal (who ever could have expected an educational factory of a thousand pupils or more to be genuinely successful?) and I responded to the teachers, all of whom knew and cared about all of us. Long before I was eight I could recite all my tables and had been promoted from the Infants to the Juniors. Here boys and girls were separated to different sections of the same building; the boys' Headmaster was Charley Burrows – balding, ancient (probably over forty), portentous of speech and manner. He was a remote figure even as he walked among us. Infractions of discipline entailed standing on the line outside his office at morning break (facing the wall, in disgrace) and being called separately into the Presence. Those last few yards were a lonely trek and his room an ogre's den. Then would come the unwanted and unnerving closeness, often followed by the grim command, 'Hold out your hand.'

Being caned on an extended palm was a double pain: the feeling of rejection was probably worse than the physical ache. Then custom demanded that you leave the room with the outraged hand tucked under the opposing armpit, the body held in a half-crouch, grimacing with pain, the mouth blowing gusts intended to convey agony bravely born. Friends entered seriously into the charade – 'How many?' – and offered to spit on the offended part. This was held to mitigate the agony.

Odd moments survive in memory, outcrops of ineradicable rock jutting above the flatland of the everyday.

During morning assembly we would sing the hymn – by heart, there being no money for hymn-books – then await the usual instruction: 'Hands together, eyes closed.' We would dutifully assume a position conventionally held to be that of prayer. Then, if it were Thursday, that invisible voice would intone, 'Now the prayer for Thursday is missing from this book, so I shall read the prayer for Saturday.' The formula never varied; he never bought a replacement book; we never even thought it odd. At certain times of the year occurred the predestined rites: Harvest Festival, Remembrance Day, Empire Day, the run up to Christmas. On Empire Day we all took Union flags, the bigger, the better, and anyone with a uniform wore it. At playtime we processed spontaneously round and round the playground, admired by the mums clustered along the railing and carrying jugs of hot cocoa and cake. There would be some kind of annual Sports Day in Kenny Gardens: most of the park was laid out with neat gravel paths circumscribing well-kept lawns with flowerbeds, with frequent notices: 'Keep off the Grass: Penalty Forty Shillings.' But the gravelly, windswept top of the reservoir was open to us and there we performed the athletic rites in which, peculiarly, sportsmen glory. It was to the Rezzy that we went on the weekly games afternoon: two piles of coats at each end did duty for goals, each of which would be guarded by a reluctant and disappointed custodian. The other twenty boys would pursue the ball like an elongated comet. Offside? Surely you jest. After the football we might stay for an illicit game in the jungle of privet which marched up and along its sloping sides, keeping an eye open for the resident guardian, Rednose the Scuffer. Even if we were detected, there were several possible avenues of escape and we were, in any case, fleet of foot: in anything like a chase his face soon assumed the colour of his nose and we would have worried for his health – had we been capable of caring.

Once a year there would be a school concert. Each class would be responsible for an item, prepared with breathless excitement and rendered on The Night with quivering determination. It was thrilling beyond words to come back to the school in the evening: darkness outside and all the lights on inside; to proffer the little square of blue cardboard, stamped with the school stamp, to Mr Kitchen. Then the opening chords of the national anthem, banged out on the piano by Mr Lewis, after which all the adults present struggled to fit themselves somehow into the school desks which were the only seating accommodation. There would be a musical item, in costume; a play – obvious children in adults' clothes, with spurious whiskers and hairdos. The girls especially, I noticed, loved dressing up. Afterwards we would disperse, having passed a vote of thanks to all concerned, nem con, and say a barrage of good-nights to Mr Kitchen again. We rarely saw the caretaker in the classrooms: he lived down in the basement where he oversaw the delivery of coke, the stoking of the boilers and the general functioning of the swimming bath which Rathbone, alone of all the schools in the neighbourhood, was fortunate to possess. The excited traipse down the cellar steps; the first breath of that damp-laden air; the first sight of that glinting and swaying surface, reflecting the gaslight from a thousand irregular facets, the bottom gleaming through. Then the race to be the first to rape that virginal intactness, the shouts echoing from the low ceiling, the later pulling-on of reluctant clothing over damp flesh, the ache in the legs as one climbed the cellar steps again. Mr Kitchen also super-vised the cleaning staff, tolled the school bell, locked and unlocked the gates, ushered visiting parents to the Headmaster's room and generally acted as the persona of the school. He was never seen out of his uniform. He had farseeing, watery eyes, a small bristle of moustache, gaunt cheekbones and a very fat wife.

Ultimately I found myself in the Scholarship Class. In those days the school leaving age was fourteen, unless you were at a grammar school, in which case it was sixteen (by when you would be expected to have matriculated), unless again you went on to the sixth form and so to a university. Fees for a grammar school were beyond the pockets of working people: eight guineas a term – a month's gross pay. But the corporation awarded a number of Junior City Scholarships annually, valid for four or five years and there was enormous competition for these all-too-rare ladders against the frequent snakes of our daily existence. In the Scholarship Class we were openly crammed for such a transition, just as turkeys are fattened for Christmas. We even had to supply two textbooks for which the school could not budget: a Longman's Arithmetic and a Pitman's English. How, eventually, my mother 'screwed out' for these, I do not know: probably the Calverts paid most or all: there was, with all the will in the world, no money to spare once my father came home to die.

The teachers live still in my memory. I wonder whether teachers generally realise their responsibility, their inescapable importance in the lives of their children. There can be few professions which bear such a burden – often an unrecognised, often a glad burden. Mr MacKay was feared as a disciplinarian, a reputation founded, it seems to me now, more on a dominating personality than on the support of punitive measures. Mr Lewis used to set, as an imposition, the writing of Sir Henry Wotton's 'Character of a Happy Life'; I still largely remember it though I have long forgotten the no doubt minor peccadilloes for which it was set. We fledglings were taught by Miss Dodd: big-boned, immensely dignified, ponderous of utterance, thorough in all that she did – and expected us to do. I am still grateful to her for reading out, in instalments, 'The Wind in the Willows', which I re-read for the umpteenth time and with undiminished enjoyment as recently as last week. She often called on us to stand up and declaim by heart passages of verse and poetry: 'A garden is a lovesome thing'; 'Admirals All'; a great deal of de la Mare; much of it I still remember. School work was an enjoyable challenge, so different from the drudgery which it later became, yet I was never competing with my fellows: rather, the challenge was to extend my own boundaries.

Outside school there was increasingly the life of the streets. We children never visited each other's homes: the thought never occurred to us; at most, we might play our games in each other's backyards. Each day fell into a routine: school; dash home for dinner and plug-in for that vital contact; school again; home from school, snatch a quick meal and dash out. Then raise your face to the heavens for an ululating, yodelling, long-drawn-out 'Oo-ed', the gang's rallying cry. It would be answered from afar, somewhere in the maze of streets, and then we would home-in on one another, howling at intervals to resume contact. Once the gang had assembled, a decision was reached, usually by some vaguely-democratic process about what we would do – though sometimes those with the loudest voices and the most aggressive stance short-circuited the process – as, in greater matters, they still do. If we had a ball, any convenient blank wall would suffice for a game of Flinchers; or a piece of chalk and a reasonably-unbusy patch of pavement were the only pre-requisites for Hopscotch – either rectangular or spiral; there could be, especially in twilight or even after dark, a wide-game; sometimes there would be a craze for whip-and-top or throwing cigarette-cards against a wall or marbles: life was certainly never boring. Today's generation, to whom that dread word is an hour-by-hour necessity are so materially blessed as to be unfortunate: in all human affairs appetite must be kept alive by scarcity. 'Is there any charm When lack from round the neck of love Drops a languid arm,' and all that. Our gang, then, drew from a wide area, an area bounded by Hall Lane, Edge Lane, Jubilee Drive and Kensington. Along the boundaries there were invisible, but real, signs, much as two pairs of robins will share a garden knowing exactly where one stretch of territory ends and another begins – a demarcation invisible to anyone else. The other side of Hall Lane was the territory of Boody Booth and his gang, whose acknowledged focus was Warburton Street; the far side of both Kensington and Edge Lane was terra incognita. Each of us carried a map within his mind with areas shaded in invisible colours: we never discussed it because it was as much a fact as the wallpaper on the bedroom wall. Ernie Edge would come up from the small dairy at the bottom of Albany Road; Douglas Scholey would arrive from the same area; Roy Christian I have mentioned; Potter Ball would arrive from Leopold Road; others would drift in from nearby. Oddly, most of them were to be killed flying, Ernie Edge as a squadron-leader, as late as the early

1950s, when the Meteor jet he was piloting went down into the Humber.

Each twilight brought a time of glamour and veiled the ugliness in mist, a mist shot through with iridescent patches of light, haloes around each glowing street-lamp. The lamplighter was a familiar figure; how dearly each of us would have loved to accompany him on his round, reaching up with his long cane and turning on the gas with the faintest of pops. Early wakers would hear his confident footsteps in the dawn-empty streets, hear them stop, see the patch of light on the ceiling fade swiftly that the uncertain daylight might assert itself. Sometimes we would chalk a goal on an end wall and take turns at being goalkeeper; inevitably, there would be the occasional crash of a breaking window, the indrawn breath of collective horror and a simultaneous and rapid dispersal in all directions. Angry householders, however fast they moved, invariably found only an innocent and empty street.

Yes, the life of the street was a full one, though not many of us realised at the time at what a cost it was being bought.

The Calverts called quite often – after all, they were family, the only family we effectively had. Often, too, I would be whisked away to spend a weekend at the huge barn which was 24 Everton Valley; before very long I would be trusted to walk down alone to Moss Street on a Friday evening and climb on to a 44 tram, alight at the end of Saint Domingo Vale and walk the last hundred yards or so to that welcome and welcoming haven. From my mother's point of view it must have been one hungry mouth less to feed for two whole days, one cause of sibling rivalry removed for the most-fraught days of the week, days when that rivalry was most likely to spill over into verbal sniping or even open warfare. How I enjoyed those weekends with the Calvert family. Each night I undressed for bed and was swathed in one of Gegga's old shirts: an adequate nightshirt for me then and such an improvement on my usual bed-going habits. Then I had to sleep on a mattress laid on the floor: an unusual and thrilling viewpoint. And, sleeping alone, there were no demarcation disputes, sometimes bitterly fought-out, in subdued tones, in the early hours of the morning – 'subdued' because if our bitter wrangling penetrated to the front bedroom swift and fearful vengeance would leave us both sobbing, all disputes forgotten. No more bony knees in the back, no getting out of bed to tuck-in again the sheets and blankets: my brother was a restless sleeper. Around the Valley there were new surroundings to explore. Walton Road was a bustling, shop-filled world with frequent trams rattling past, a world from which I absorbed unconsciously new vitality. There were the wide expanses of Stanley Park: a very savannah of open grass, with a lake, and boats. On Saturdays we might climb on to a tram and ride down to the Pier Head or even as far as the wide sands of Seaforth. And the Calverts possessed a wireless, a crystal set: you put on earphones and somebody juggled with a catswhisker: tinny voices flickered within your head. One day I heard some opera: I recall it yet. It was, and I made quite, quite certain that I remembered, an aria called 'Home to our Mountains,' and it was part of Il Trovatore. There and then I added yet another resolve to the accumulating total: this was yet another scout, come to meet me from a better world, a world into which I would one day enter. I did, indeed, though it was to be many years and many deaths away. Already, then, I had glimpsed unlimited space, full of growing things; there were aeroplanes to drift overhead; now there was opera. What else was there still to come?

The Calverts possessed a small store of books and these I read avidly, many of them repeatedly: all the 'William' books, 'Three men in a Boat', 'King Solomon's Mines', the 'Boats of the Glen Carrig' (is this eerie masterpiece still extant?), the 'Lances of Lynwood'. One glorious day, I remember, I found the 'Thirty-nine Steps' of John Buchan. I started reading just after breakfast and for the whole of that day resisted all efforts to get me to open my eyes again in the real world. I refused lunch and attempts to get me to go out, and it was only when I had laid the book down, with a deep sigh of utter content, that I even thought about tea. Few books in a life of much reading have had so great an effect on me: I suppose it was the right book at precisely the right time. On a Saturday evening, disregarding the queue outside the long-vanished Lyric Theatre, opposite, we would often go to the Garrick cinema nearby and climb the long, steep staircase to the gods. The Garrick was unique: instead of a ticket you were handed a metal disc with a hole at the centre and this was collected by the attendant and threaded on to a string, for later return to the box-office. It was at the Garrick that I saw 'The Phantom of the Opera', the original version with Douglas Fairbanks and Mary Pickford. I accepted completely, as indeed we all did, the wholly-unlikely concept of a room whose spiked ceiling would lower at villainous will to spear the heroine in a dozen places. I remember the relief when, by the superhuman intervention of the hero, the spikes were arrested, quivering, even as they disturbed the very fabric tightly stretched over that innocent bosom. We accepted the conventions of the time as today's audiences accept a different, and nastier, set. Then on Sunday evenings it was a reluctant walk to the tram and a slow journey home through the darkness. Sleepers Hill, Nether-field Road, past the Collegiate School (as yet, only a landmark). Then Moss Street again, and the grasping arms of everyday life had practically seized me once more. Finally the long walk up Prescot Street and home – a home which contained Mum, true, but a home which did not revolve around me, where I was forced to compete, if unknowingly, with my siblings for a share of our over-worked mother.

It must have been about now that the neighbourhood buzzed with our own, home-grown, ghost-story. It was a story which fuelled endless jangling sessions. In one of the narrow streets off Bowler Street – cobbled alleyways with opposing houses no more than twenty feet apart – a man committed suicide. I know not why: the area and the time were littered with plenty of convincing reasons for suicide, which must often and to many people have seemed to make more sense than trying to carry on a futile existence. So one night this anonymous man cut his throat in the back bedroom of the house in which he was lodging. For a time the house was a place of ghoulish pilgrimage: local children stared openly, expecting they knew not what. Our own gang went over there one evening but could create little in the way of horror in that prosaic street. The widow whose home it was cleaned up the mess, attended the inquest, was almost the sole mourner at the funeral; later she advertised for another lodger, but a response was long in coming. One afternoon she was sitting, according to local custom, on the top doorstep, blocking the doorway. Practically every such doorway held just such a female figure; it seems to me, now, that the scene called out for some local Lowry. The women were occupied gossiping across the narrow street while keeping an eye on the many pre-school children wringing interest out of their squalid surroundings. Suddenly a neighbour, directly opposite the widow, saw her levitated from the doorstep, still in a sitting conformation, and deposited ungently some feet further forward. Simultaneously she started to scream. From all directions women ran to her; children, disturbed, clustered wide-eyed a little further away. When her hysterics had been allayed, she managed to tell the others that she had become conscious of footsteps coming down the stairs behind her and advancing down the narrow hallway. Even as it dawned on her that she was – or should have been – alone in the house, she felt herself picked up, propelled forwards and dropped. Something went past and was gone. The story was retold endlessly, the details being polished ever-smoother, like any water-worn pebble. Whatever had happened, it never happened again but that occupant soon left and the house stood empty for several months. Finally it was taken by a tenant who believed nothing of the wild tales told to her, nor did she ever have cause to modify her opinions.

It was our only brush with the supernatural, unless the legends of Spring Heel Jack were also to be catalogued under this head. Jack was said to be humanoid, with glowing eyes and menacing teeth, able to jump from rooftop to rooftop – he was never reported at ground level – and always surrounded by an aura of infernal light, reinforced by the darkness in which he usually chose to appear. In later years I was to find that the legend surfaced in other places: a soldier on sentry-go on Salisbury Plain was said not only to have seen him but to have fired at him, though without apparent effect. Whenever we went out at night, for a time, we lived in dreadful hope of seeing Jack, but the rooftops, anxiously scanned, showed only wet slates glistening in the occasional moonlight. Some of our legends were living and tangible – if, indeed, we had dared touch. Regularly past our house went a peculiar couple: a young-old man, shabbily-dressed, humming unmusically, with distant, vacant eyes. As he walked, his right hand lifted and fell as regularly as though he were a mechanical toy; the hand held what appeared to be a piece of bone which he raised to his lips and lowered and raised and lowered. His left arm was locked to the right arm of the woman once hired as an escort and now herself driven past the accepted borders of sanity by the daily companionship of that mindless other. We watched, shuddered and worked at forgetting. Then, further down Edge Lane was a Mormon church, standing in its own grounds behind a high wall. Local women spoke of it in whispers that we children might not overhear; local girls were forbidden to pass it without crossing to the other side of the road. It was a place of mystery and horror, the worse for being nameless and unexplained, though clearly potent. Our mother refused to answer questions about it, with a decided air of I-have-a-tale-to-tell-if-only-I-dared-tell-it. And, of course, Boody Booth's gang spread apprehension, though I think we created that fear from the minimum of evidence. Certainly, poverty-stricken or not, the streets were infinitely safer to walk at night than they are now.

Why, I wonder, did we need so to create terror for ourselves? As a counterweight to the miseries of the everyday? Or to satisfy some need for the numinous, a need not satisfied by the various forms of institutional religion available to us? Certainly, at all ages we delighted in horrors. Among us children there were innumerable grisly anecdotes: for a new one, you could be sure of an attentive audience: fingernails found in pork pies (we had not heard of Sweeney Todd); corpses galore; footsteps where nothing was to be seen. At night, alone, even on the familiar staircase of home and even more so in the equally-familiar street, each of us walked in solitary fear.

Like one that on a lonesome road
Doth walk in fear and dread,
And having once turned round walks on
And turns no more his head,
Because he knows a frightful fiend
Doth close behind him tread.

My own progress upstairs, along the landing and around the bend to our bedroom, holding a candle to keep the encroaching shadows at bay, would have been comical to a beholder: my head went round and round like an occulting lighthouse.

Daylight brought its share of occasional diversions. I can still remember the General Strike of 1926: a procession of striking miners came up the Lane behind a band; there was a banner; they turned around just beneath our windows and went back again. The newspaper was decidedly peculiar, a single sheet, I seem to remember. In later years, on two separate occasions graceful airships passed slowly overhead, the sun glinting on the ribbed envelopes. One, I suppose, was the Hindenburg and the other the R100; the one was destroyed by an unforeseen disaster and the other by political spite and jealousy. Almost opposite us was some kind of working men's club; we knew of it only that a prodigious amount of beer was drunk there: the mountains of empties testified to that. Sometimes we were aroused from our first precarious sleep by shouts of incoherent rage as the members spilled out at closing time. Incomprehensible words were uttered, words which we suspected shrewdly we should not ask Mother about. We would erupt from bed and kneel at the window, watching, overlooking the shivers of cold in that unheated room. The eager bystanders beneath us would press outwards to leave an irregular arena, in which the opponents – grown men – would belabour one another. We enjoyed the drama, the raw emotion, and were disappointed when spectators dragged the contestants apart and led them away. Or during the evening some thirsty and poverty-stricken soul would insert one foot in the door of the public bar opposite and launch out in song. Such songs were almost always Irish, whatever that proves: 'The Rose of Tralee', 'Danny Boy', 'The Wearing of the Green'. Later the singer would enter and seek a reward; as he rarely came out for some time, I can only assume that such an appeal to boozy charity rarely failed. When the crowds reluctantly spilled out at ten o'clock or so, there would inevitably be a performance of Liverpool's civic anthem: 'Nellie Dean'. The pubs in the Lane were so close together that in the still night air it was perfectly possible for the clientele of several pubs to sing in unison without going a step nearer to each other. Such a chorus would always be unharmonious and hardly in perfect synchronisation. In the evenings directly preceding an election even the children caught the excitement. We would parade the streets in ragged processions, bearing sticks with election cards, banging tin cans, singing raucously:

> Vote, vote, vote for Bessie Braddock
> Throw old Jackson in the dock.
> For our Braddock is the man
> And we'll have her if we can...

Try as I might, the last line escapes me: after all, it is fifty-odd years ago. If, by the way, you detect any logical flaw in the chant, we certainly didn't. Bessie was large – 'beaucoup de monde sur le balcon', as the French so gracefully put it (the Germans call it a high waterfall: readers of present-day tabloids would, no doubt, put it more crudely) and a warrior manquée. If the evening newspaper, the *Echo*, appeared with large placards saying 'Disgraceful scene in council chamber', then we knew that Bessie had again crossed the floor and dragged one of her opponents out of her seat by the hair. There was a classic occasion when a joker put an advertisement in the *Echo*: 'For sale, one pair of trousers hardly worn. Owner has no use for them.' At the end was the name of Bessie's husband, a more prosaic city councillor, in the same political interest as his wife. He would, I suppose, hardly have dared be otherwise.

The highspot of the year, in many respects, was July 12th. This date is the anniversary of the Battle of the Boyne, though what the battle might have been about, few of us knew. On that day every year an endless succession of marching bands – drum and fife, or concertina, or pipe, or occasionally a full brass band, processed along all the converging arteries to the city centre. Once there they blocked by their presence all traffic despite the efforts of hoarse and sweating policemen. Each lodge featured a King Billy in seventeenth-century costume, full-bottomed wig down over his shoulders. This gentleman was sometimes astride a horse and was given, in any case, to waving a naked sword around his head. There would be a hefty male carrying a cushion on which reposed an open Bible. Around these two main characters would be the children, clad in white with orange sashes, the women in their very best, and the men, all in blue serge suits and inevitably wearing bowlers. It was usually de rigeur for each man to carry a rolled umbrella tightly clamped under the left arm; later in the day this served as a useful weapon and rumour said that there were often unorthodox additions to the umbrella, discreetly hidden by the sober wrappings. There would be a huge and colourful banner carried between two hefty men, with dependent silk cords held symbolically by favoured acolytes. Altogether there would be several thousand marchers. They would either climb into a special train at Exchange Station and go for a day at Southport, or they would carry on to the Landing Stage and depart for New Brighton. That evening they would all return, form up and start the long trek home. By now the police, reinforced with many men on horseback, would be out in great force. Many of the shop windows on the route would now be boarded up. There would be expectant crowds, all experiencing the first frissons of empathetic excitement. The crowds would be greatest in the vicinity of Pembroke Place, where the lodges would diverge: some for Wavertree and some for Old Swan or Netherfield Road. The marching men would show evident signs of the day's celebrations: here a bowler hat flataback, there a loosened tie, an occasional discord or a wayward stagger. Lurking in sidestreets along the route, and especially in the Pembroke Place area, would be groups of the opposition, mainly Irish Catholics – as great bigots in their way as the Orange-men in theirs. None of us who witnessed that annual and diverting spectacle have been in the slightest surprised at recent and undiverting horrors in Ulster. As the procession made its way along Dale Street there would be occasional scuffles, deftly snuffed out by the police. But in the open space of Pembroke Place the police found it more difficult to keep the two groups apart. Then battle would be joined, a three-cornered battle of Catholics, Orangemen and police. As the battle swayed unpredictably this way and that, excitement seekers would inevitably get caught up in it and would struggle frantically to avoid rearing horses, trun-cheons and struggling men. It was all great fun – except, perhaps, to God, in whose Name all this was (in theory) happening. To us children, however, it was a free, colourful, dramatic and exciting spectacle.

About now – would it have been 1930? – some kind of civic anniversary came round and it was decided that Liverpool should at last make an honest woman (as the quaint saying used to be) of the Mersey by means of some formal nuptials. There seemed to be no way of asking the River Mersey for its opinion on this and silence was read as acquiescence: how wrong our local bigwigs were. Accordingly, one Sunday afternoon two ferries left the Landing Stage; they were gaily beflagged and on the first of the two a band was playing on the open deck. That boat was crammed with what are laughingly known to any local paper as civic dignitaries: aldermen and councillors, with spouses, heads of various municipal undertakings and local voluntary bodies; all the usual stuffed and worthy shirts who normally appear on platforms, attend free functions and get their pictures in the local paper. The second boat largely carried their understrappers, and preserved a seemly distance, steaming – as it were – at heel. Having arrived at a position roughly midway between Egremont Pier and the Gladstone Dock, the two ships pointed their bows into the tide and maintained steerage way only. Churchmen of all denominations then played their part; the Lady Mayoress, Miss Margaret Bevan as I recall, made a speech with many historical and civic references,